SOUND LIKE A SMART CREATOR

JOHN SCOTT

Copyright © 2024 John Scott
Illustrations copyright © 2024 John Scott

Visit the author's website at john.studio

All rights reserved.

No part of this publication may be reproduced,
distributed, or transmitted in any form or
by any means, including photocopying,
recording, or other electronic or mechanical
methods, without the prior written permission
of the author.

Written by John Scott
Illustrated by John Scott
Cover Design by John Scott
Copyright Page by John Scott
New Book Smell provided by John Scott

First Edition: Dec 2024
Published by Milo & Mose Media

Printed in the United States of America

For my 3 reasons why.

lightbulb moment
noun (informal)

A moment of sudden realization, enlightenment, or inspiration.

THE GOAL OF THIS BOOK

Have you ever been listening to a podcast, and the guest says something so profound it makes you think - **"Damn! They smart!"** I know I have.. So often, in fact, that I felt situations like these deserved a name. I call these little epiphanies, *Lightbulb Moments.*

If you don't know what I'm talking about, just scroll through YouTube shorts or TikTok until you see a podcast clip pop up. You'll see what I mean. Anyway, at some point I started making a list of these moments so I could memorize them and be able to drop these knowledge bombs any time I wanted.

That way people will think *ME* smart.

So.. In an effort to impact others the same way these smart creators have impacted me, I've turned that lightbulb list into a book to share with you.

So now... *WE* smart.

EXAMPLES

soundsm.art/lightbulb1   soundsm.art/lightbulb2   soundsm.art/lightbulb3

HOW TO USE THIS BOOK

While this book started as a list I wanted to memorize, turning it into a book has helped me do just that. But lucky for you, there is a much easier way to memorize everything in this book.. and that's called...

SPACED REPETITION

Spaced repetition is reviewing something you learn at increasing intervals to improve long-term retention.

Basically, you learn something new, take a little break, review it, take a longer break, review it again, take an even LONGER break, you get the idea.

Studies have shown that with spaced repetition, many people achieve perfect recall within a few weeks.

I kept this book to around 50 or so concepts (with a few extras at the end), so within a month, you should be ready to blow people's minds the next time someone asks you to be on their podcast.

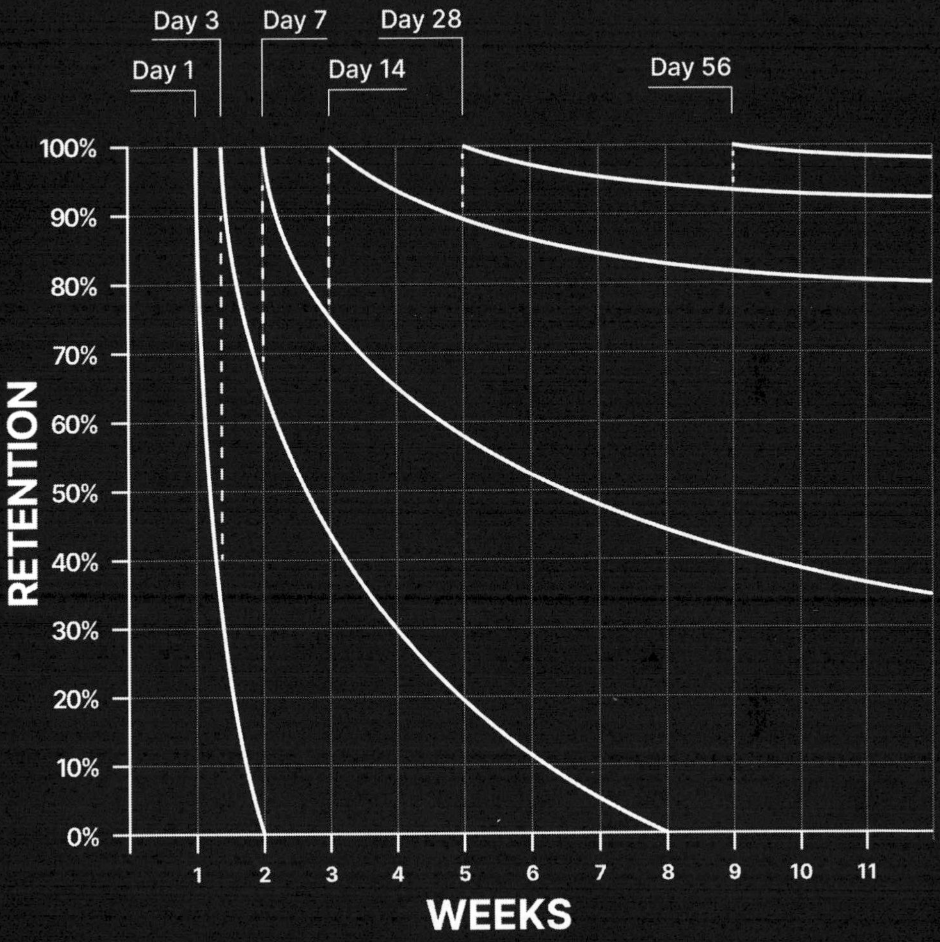
Day 1
Day 3
Day 7
Day 14
Day 28
Day 56
100%
90%
80%
70%
60%
50%
40%
30%
20%
10%
0%
RETENTION
1
2
3
4
5
6
7
8
9
10
11
WEEKS

READING WHILE LISTENING

Multiple studies have shown that reading while listening (RWL) improves understanding and retention of the material being read.

When I personally listen to audio books, I probably grasp about 50% of the info. The other 50%? I don't know what you'd call it but it's like..

Productive daydreaming? I'll have epiphanies, brainstorm content ideas, come up with random-ass marketing strategies.. which is great and all but I usually have to start chapters over because of it.

I can't even tell you how long it took me to get through Gary Vaynerchuk's *Day Trading Attention*. The dude would say something, my gears would start turning and before I knew it, the book would be over.

So, since this book is a bit shorter than your average novel, I whipped up an audio version with some added content. Fun facts, extra examples, personal stories, pro tips, creator hacks.. everything you get in this book, but just a bit more.

So if you want to memorize this book even faster, here is a link to the audio version. ⟶

soundsm.art/audiobook

ALL RIGHT, ENOUGH BULLSHIT.
IT'S TIME TO SOUND SMART

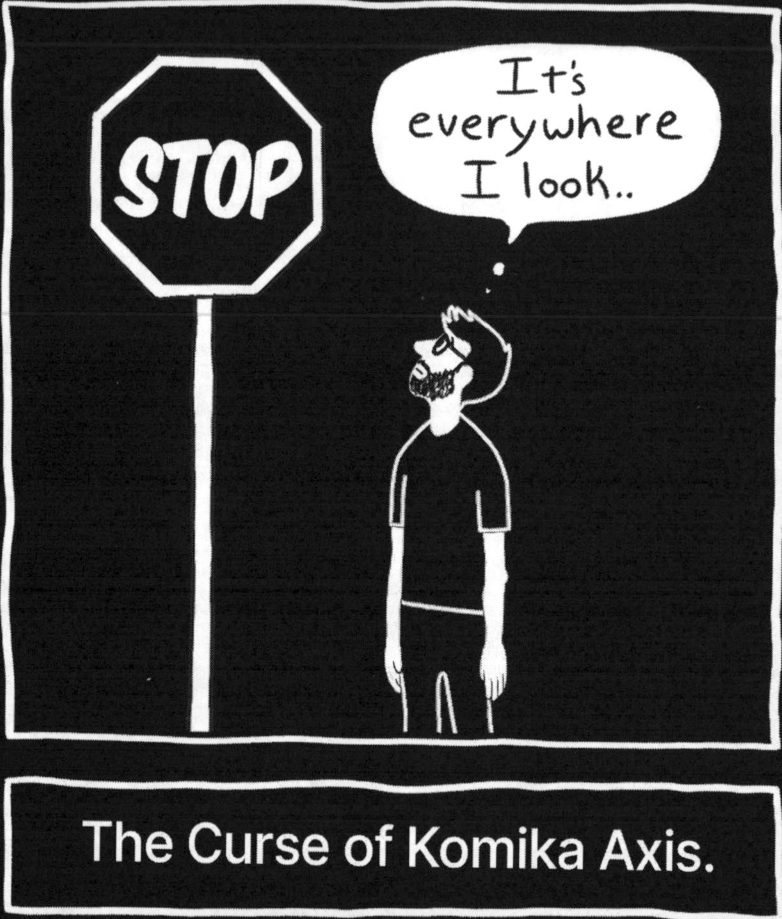
STOP
It's everywhere I look..
The Curse of Komika Axis.

Frequency Illusion

(Baader-Meinhof phenomenon)

Once you learn about something new, you start noticing it everywhere.

ORIGIN

In 1994, St. Paul, MN resident Terry Muller wrote to his local paper describing an odd experience. He said that ever since he'd first heard about the German terrorist group, *Baader-Meinhof*, he suddenly saw them mentioned everywhere. Once published, a ridiculous amount of readers reported the same experience.

CAUSES

1. **Selective Attention** - They become more aware of it. (Pg. 51)
2. **Confirmation Bias** - Each time it happens = suspicion confirmed. (Pg.81)

EXAMPLES

- When you learn a new word, you might notice a lot more people using it.
- After getting a new car, you might start seeing that model everywhere.
- When you see a specific font used by a big YouTuber, you might start seeing it being used by **EVERY FREAKING CHANNEL WHY THE HELL IS EVERYONE USING KOMIKA AXIS FUUUUUUUUUU**

(Sorry for all caps, I rewrote that part to match the audio book)

Fitts' Law

*The closer or bigger something is,
the faster you can click it.*

ORIGIN

In 1954, psychologist Paul Fitts came up with a model to explain how we can interact with things faster if they're bigger or closer to us. Duh, right? Well.. as obvious as that might sound, I looked into his research, and..

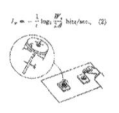

I'm not even gonna pretend to understand all that, but it did open my eyes to something: Things that seem obvious today, like bigger buttons being clicked faster.. weren't always so clear.. We didn't ALWAYS have tiny computers in our pockets.

Pro Tip (Web Designers): If you're designing a website or a landing page, make sure the button you want clicked (like "Buy Now" or "Sign Up") is right where the visitor's thumb already is.

Examples: 1. soundsm.art/fittslaw1 2. soundsm.art/fittslaw2 3. soundsm.art/fittslaw3

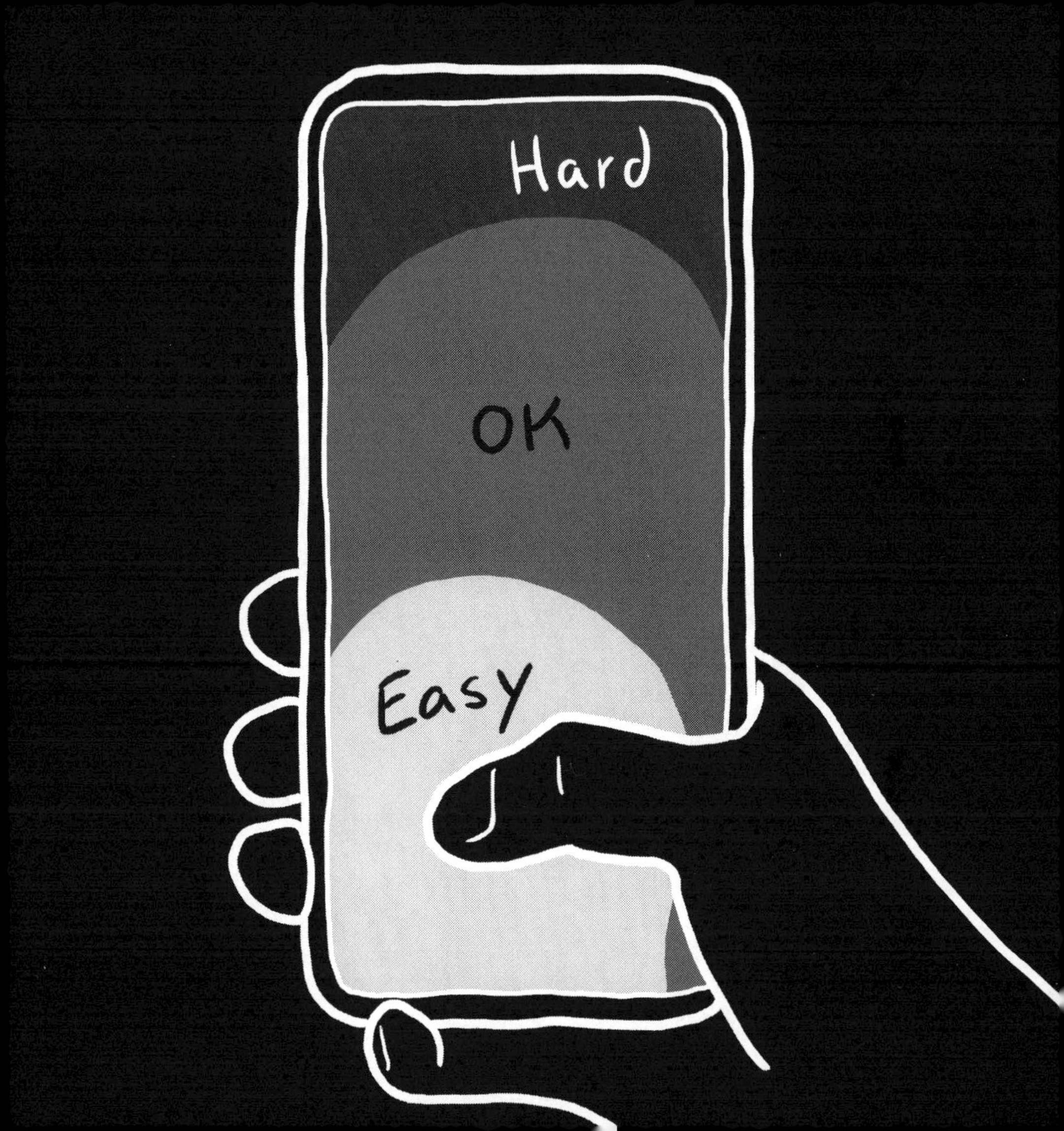
Hard
OK
Easy

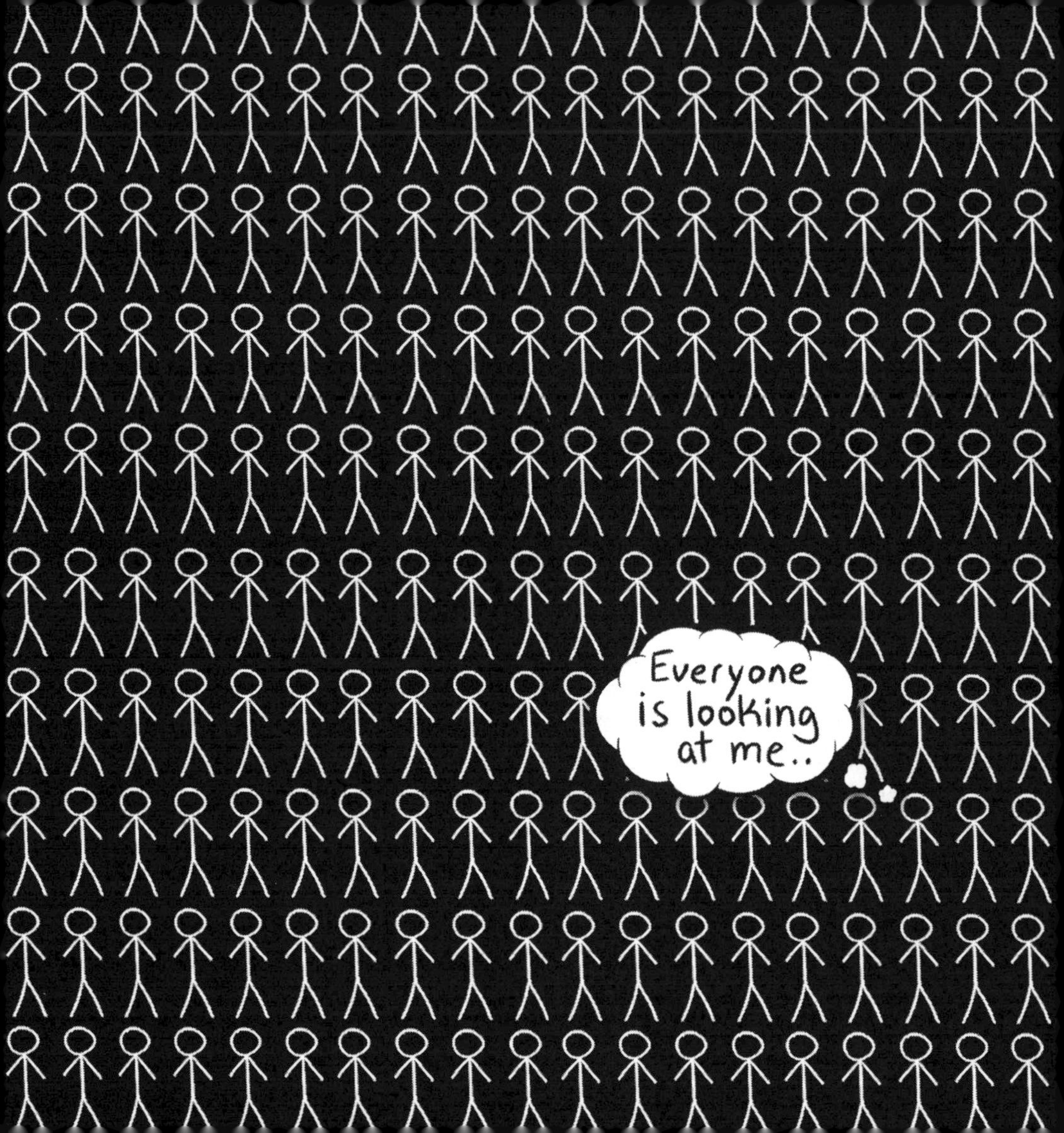
Everyone is looking at me..

Spotlight Effect

We overestimate how much others notice us.

ORIGIN

In a 2000 experiment, psychologists Thomas Gilovich, Victoria Husted Medvec, and Kenneth Savitsky had participants wear an embarrassing t-shirt and then estimate how many people would notice them. They guessed that around 50% of people would notice the shirt they were wearing but in reality, only about 25% did.

The T-Shirt had Barry Manilow on it. Barry Manilow is a singer who was pretty popular in the 70s. I guess not so much in the early 2000s.

FYI - NO ONE CARES

'Remembering that embarrassing thing you did 5 years ago.' is a popular meme because it's so relatable.

So why is there no *'Remembering that embarrassing thing **your friend** did 5 years ago.'* meme?

People pay attention to themselves more than anyone else. We instinctively analyze our behavior for the same reason we learn not to touch a hot stove.. Self preservation. Your brain is wired to focus on that thing you did 5 years ago but most likely, you're the only one that remembers it.

Paradox of Choice

More choices can lead to decision paralysis.

ORIGIN

Psychologist Barry Schwartz coined the term 'Paradox of Choice' in his 2004 book, *The Paradox of Choice: Why More is Less*. In it, he writes about the *Jam Study*, conducted by psychologists Sheena Iyengar and Mark Lepper.

In their experiment, shoppers were presented with either 6 or 24 varieties of jam. While more people were attracted to the larger display, those exposed to fewer options were significantly more likely to make a purchase, suggesting that too many choices can overwhelm consumers.

EXAMPLES

1. When the shampoo brand Head & Shoulders decreased their product options from 26 down to 15, their revenue increased by 10%.

2. A psychological study found that 401(k) participation rates dropped by 10% when employees had 35 investment options compared to only 5.

Pro Tip (Content Creators): Keep Call-To-Actions clear, and singular. Asking someone to subscribe, check out your Patreon *and* sign up for your newsletter all at once will overwhelm and probably annoy them.

Time spent deciding: 56min
Your Next Watch
Continue Watching
New

Me right now using the Generation Effect to memorize the Generation Effect
Generation Effect
You rememb

Generation Effect

You remember information better if you generate it yourself, rather than just reading it.

ORIGIN

In 1970, there was a psychological study where participants were shown the first letter of a word and its opposite, while other participants were shown the same thing but with letters missing so they could fill in the blank.

Group 1	Group 2
HOT, COLD	**HOT, C___**

After a significant amount of time had passed with other studies in between, the participants that had to fill in the blank (group 2) recalled that information much easier than the participants who simply read the information.

META EXAMPLE

Right now I'm trying to write the definitions in this book from memory. If I get them right, the Generation Effect will help my brain lock in that information. It's all about actively engaging with the material. Creating your own flashcards, taking notes in your own words, and teaching others what you've learned can all work just as well. (The best technique is on Pg. 102)

End of History Illusion

The belief that we've changed a lot up to now, but won't change much in the future.

ORIGIN

In a study of over 19,000 people aged 18 to 68, participants underestimated how much they'd change in the next decade. For example, 30-year-olds expected a tiny bit of change to come, but 40-year-olds reported significant changes since they were 30.

In 2013, these findings were published by psychologists Jordi Quoidbach, Daniel Gilbert, and Timothy Wilson in Science magazine.

Now.. In the words of Fred Durst..

JUST THINK ABOUT IT

Would you say you're more mature now than you were 10 years ago? Have you grown a lot as a person? Do you think you from 10 years back could have guessed that *this* is who you would be today? I know my dumbass couldn't have.

Now think about you 10 years from now. Doesn't it kinda feel like you'll be the same person as you are today? Crazy. We be changing tho.

|———————————|————————|
Past · Lots of change · Now · Never gonna change again · Future

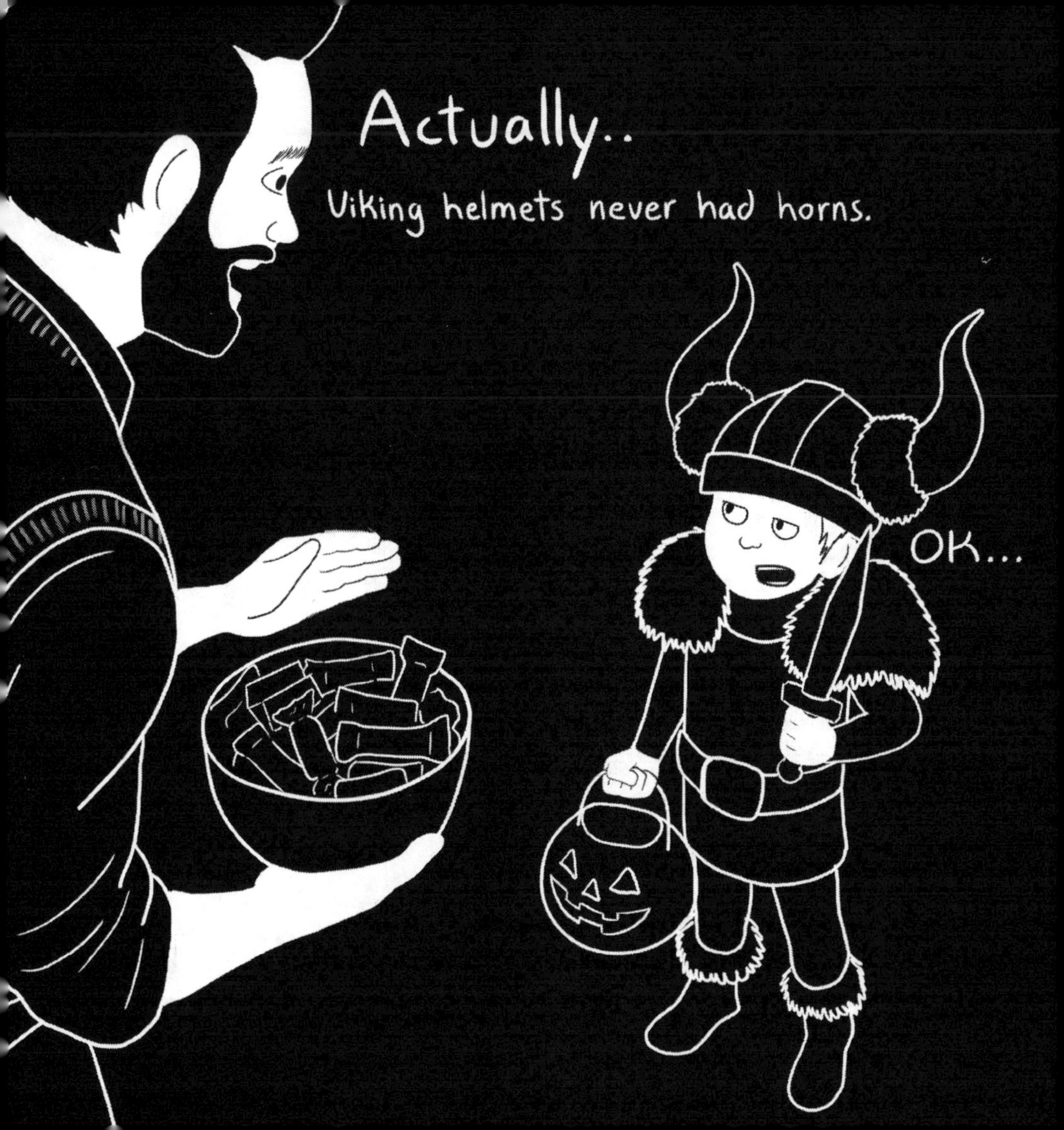
Actually..
Viking helmets never had horns.
OK...

Hypercorrection Effect

When you remember something better after you've been corrected on it.

ORIGIN

In 2001, psychologists Janet Metcalfe and Brady Butterfield used neuroimaging to observe that the medial frontal cortex of the brain becomes much more active when people receive unexpected corrections on information they *thought* they knew. So, while something learned can easily be lost, being wrong about something ain't so easy to forget.

EXAMPLE

This dude will never eat meatballs again.

soundsm.art/hypercorrection

SPOILER ALERT

When I was a kid, my Dad told me that the star of a movie never dies. So one day, my brother and I get in an argument because he says that the main character DOES die in *Armageddon*. I was so confident in what Dad had told me, I bet my brother $5.00 that he was wrong. So we watched it and yeah.. Bruce Willis let 11-year-old me down. Thanks a lot, Dad.

(**Side Note:** My brother had seen it before so he let me keep my money.)

Functional Fixedness

Struggling to see any other use for an object outside its intended purpose.

ORIGIN

In his 1945 experiment, Karl Duncker gave participants a candle, matches, and a box of thumbtacks. He asked them to attach the candle to a wall so it wouldn't drip onto the table. Most struggled as they tried to tack the candle to the wall or use melted wax to glue it to the wall somehow. Only a few participants tacked the box to the wall to hold the candle.

Funny enough, participants that were presented with the tacks outside of the box were twice as likely to solve the problem. (Because it looked like 4 items instead of 3.)

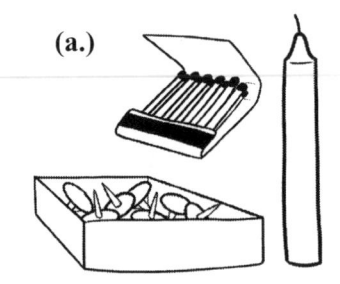

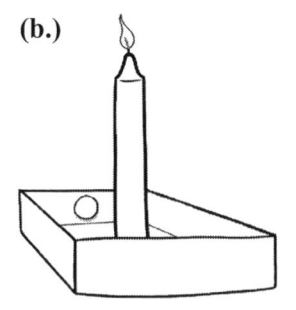

EXAMPLE

A hammer is much more than a tool for hitting nails.. It can easily be a paper weight if you're so inclined. lol

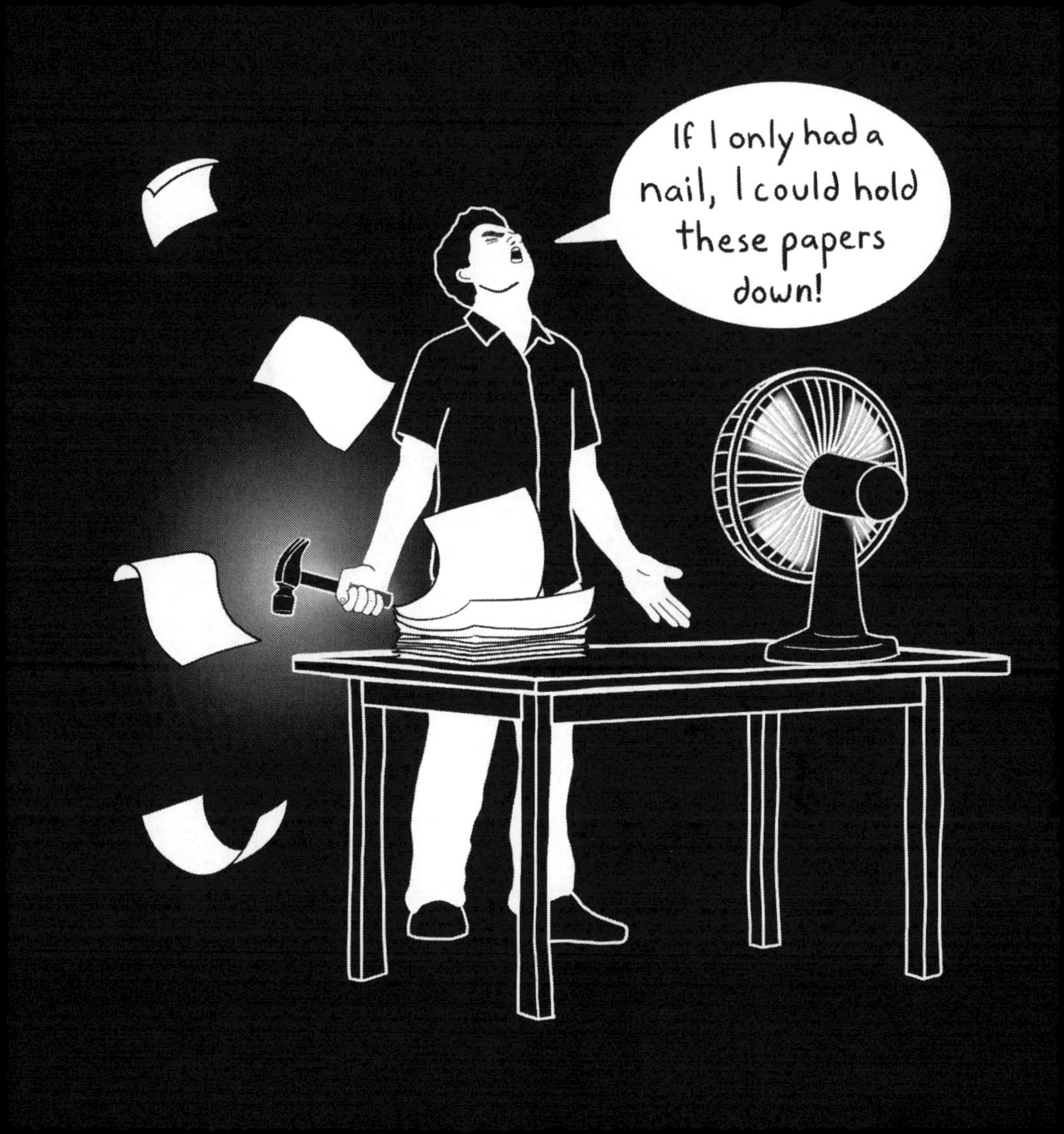
If I only had a nail, I could hold these papers down!

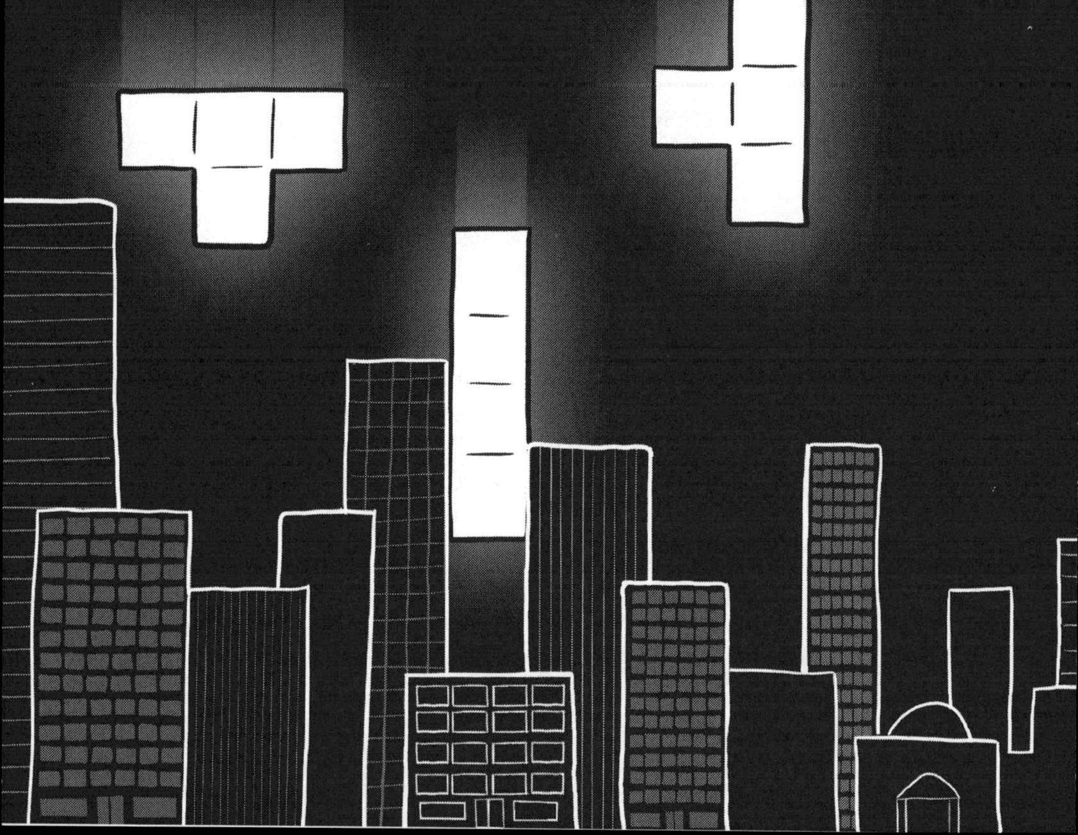

Tetris Effect

When you focus on something so much that it starts shaping how you see the world.

ORIGIN

Beginning in 1994, research has shown that people who played Tetris for extended periods started seeing Tetris shapes in their dreams and everyday life. Participants also experienced hypnagogic imagery, which is when you close your eyes and still have visualizations.

What's really crazy is that participants with amnesia, who couldn't remember playing Tetris at all, *still* experienced these visualizations.

NOT ONLY TETRIS

One of the researchers, Stickhold, reported 'feeling the rocks' as he drifted off to sleep after a long day of rock climbing. Software developers have reported dreaming about code. Artists who immerse themselves in new projects begin noticing patterns, colors, and shapes in their environment that they had not previously recognized. *Side note: This can actually cause something called the* **Frequency Illusion** (Pg. 11)

Fun Fact: Because of how Tetris affects the brain, new research shows that it could be used to prevent the formation of traumatic memories and PTSD.

Rhyme as Reason Effect

People perceive rhyming statements as more truthful and memorable.

ORIGIN

In 1999, psychologists Matthew S. McGlone and Jessica Tofighbakhsh investigated how the aesthetic quality of rhyming influences the perceived truthfulness of statements.

In their experiments, participants evaluated the accuracy of sayings that rhymed and sayings that did not. When "What sobriety conceals, alcohol reveals" was compared to the non-rhyming version "What sobriety conceals, alcohol unmasks.", participants consistently rated the rhyming version as more accurate.

EXAMPLES

Advertising: Research indicates that rhyming slogans and jingles drive more business. ♪ *NATIONWIDE IS ON YOUR SIDE* ♪

Legal Arguments: The use of rhyming in the O.J. Simpson trial, "If the glove doesn't fit, you must acquit" made their argument feel more legit.

(Rhyme not intended)

Your water's green because it's clean!
I don't know why, but I believe him..

McDammits Drive-Thru

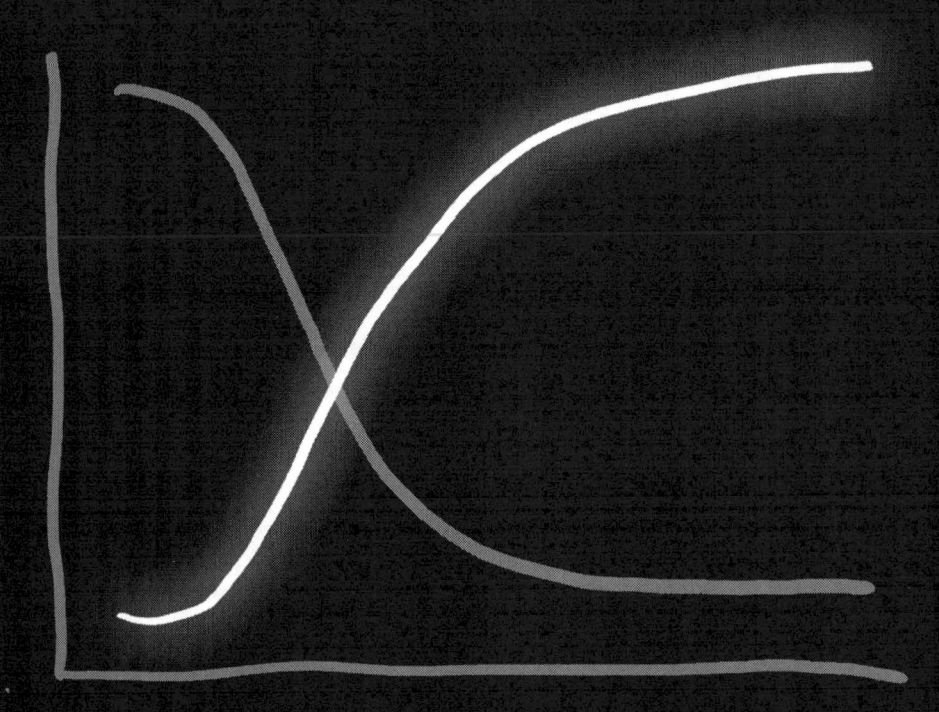

Average Drive-thru Time
# of mistakes

Goodhart's Law

*When a measure becomes a target,
it ceases to be a good measure.*

ORIGIN

In 1975, British economist Charles Goodhart noticed that whenever the government set a specific target to improve the economy, people would just game the system to hit the target without actually helping anything. He wrote about this concept and it forever became known as 'Goodhart's Law'

STORYTIME

In the late 1980s, the Soviet Union faced a nail shortage. To solve this problem, factories were offered bonuses based on the number of nails they could produce. Factories responded to this offer by making millions of tiny, useless nails so they could get their bonuses.

After seeing these tiny crappy nails, the government decided to change the bonus target to the **weight** of nails instead.

Once the factories got the news, they started cranking out huge, heavy nails instead. They met the target, got the bonuses and the government was left with gigantic nails that were just as useless.

Barnum Effect

When people think general statements apply specifically to them.

ORIGIN

In 1948, psychologist Bertram R. Forer ran an experiment with his students. He gave them personality tests and handed out "personalized" descriptions based on their results.

Except.. They **WEREN'T** personalized.. Not only were all of those descriptions the exact same as each other, but he copied them directly from horoscopes.

When he asked the students how accurate the results were on a scale of 0 to 5, the rating averaged out to 4.26.

Dude got 4 out of 5 stars just by gaslighting everyone.

He named this concept after P.T. Barnum, an American showman/entrepreneur famous for his promotion style and hoaxes. He's the guy that's credited with the saying *"There's a sucker born every minute."*

Fun Fact: No newspaper has ever printed a retraction for an incorrect horoscope.

Opportunity
Awaits you

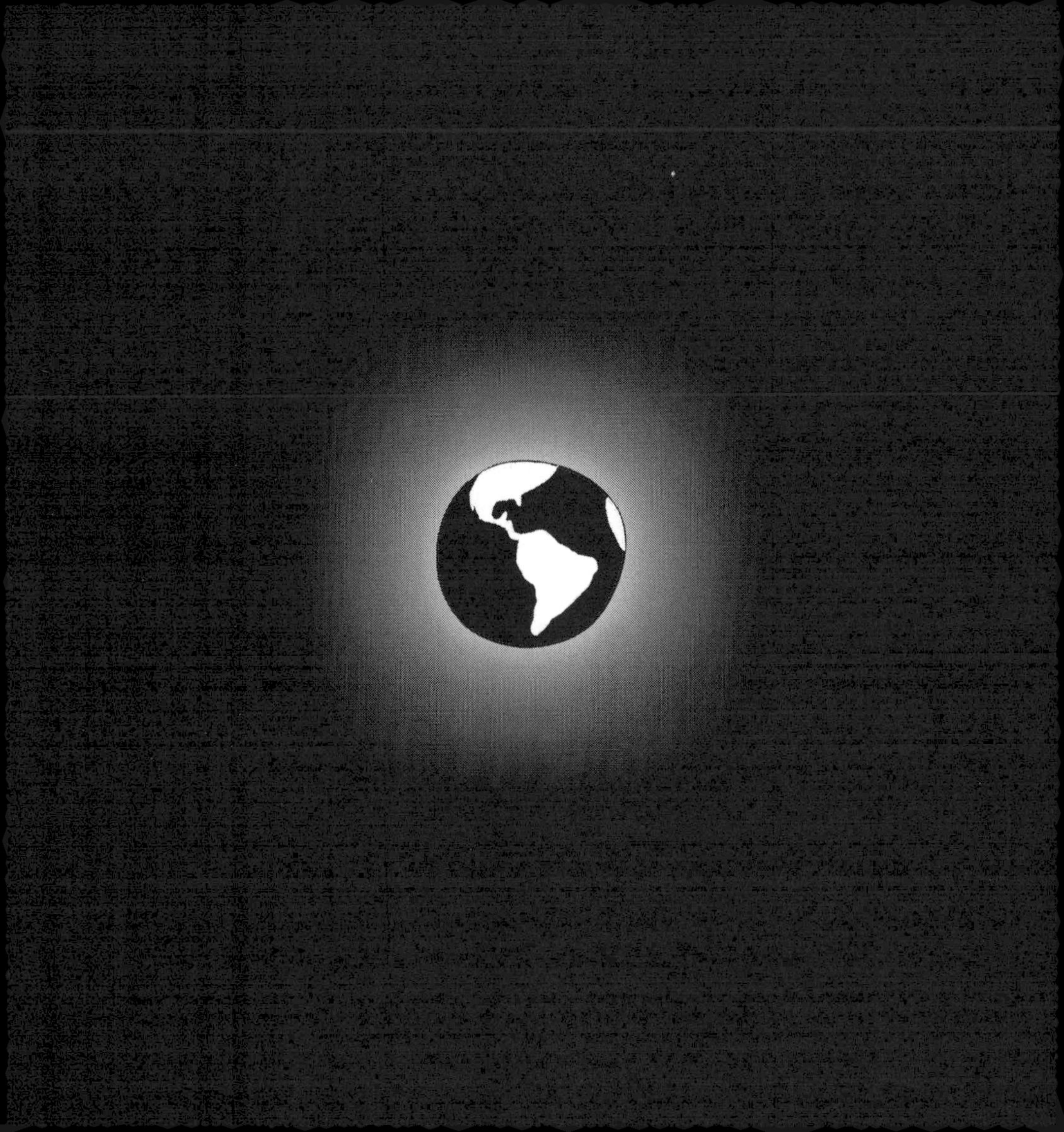

Overview Effect

A shift in perspective astronauts experience when viewing Earth from space, realizing its fragility and unity.

ORIGIN

In 1987, author Frank White found that many astronauts reported a profound change in how they viewed Earth and humanity after seeing the planet from space. They said they realized how fragile it is, how all life is connected, and how insignificant borders actually are.

Got 3 minutes?
Do yourself a favor.

Carl Sagan's
Pale Blue Dot

soundsm.art/bluedot

BADASS QUOTE:

From out there on the moon, international politics look so petty. You want to grab a politician by the scruff of the neck and drag him a quarter of a million miles out and say, "Look at that, you son of a bitch."

-Edgar Mitchell (Astronaut, obviously)

Dunbar's Number

The theory that humans can maintain only about 150 stable social relationships.

ORIGIN

In the 1990s, anthropologist Robin Dunbar proposed that humans have a cognitive limit to the number of meaningful relationships they can manage.

He basically said (over-simplified and horribly paraphrased):

'Here is an ape's brain, they can have X many relationships.
Here is a human brain, it has evolved over time, so X grows into Y.'

..And yeah.. *$Y=150$*.

MODERN EXAMPLES

Dunbar's Number can actually be observed in social media, workplaces, and even military units, where teams are often kept small to strengthen bonds and communication.

If it's not obvious already, I've never found Dunbar's Number particularly interesting, but I have heard probably hundreds of smart creators talk about it so yeah.. 150.

Meaningful Relationships

150

Friends

50

Good Friends

15

Close Relationships

5

Me

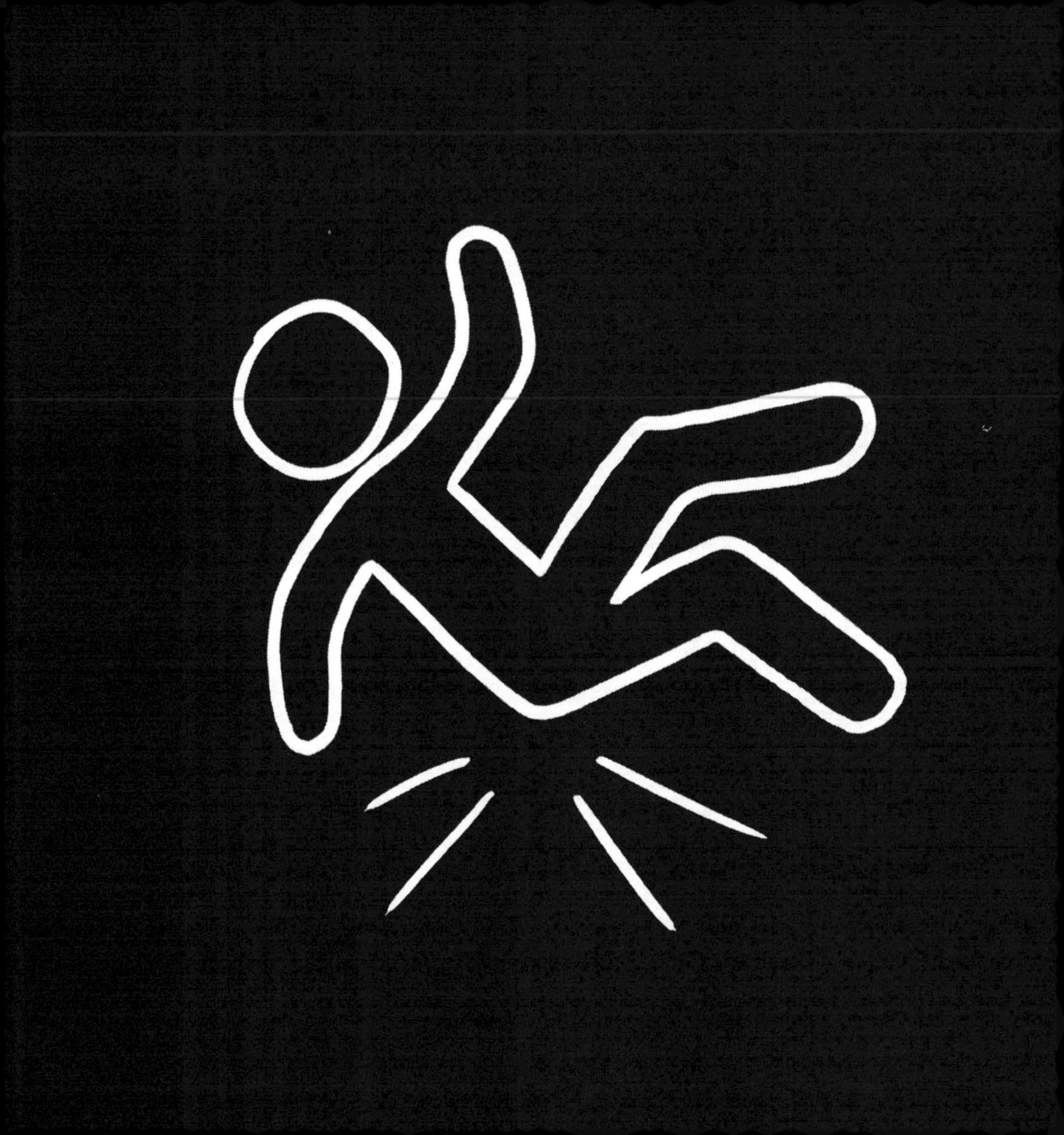

Pratfall Effect

Making a mistake can actually make you more likable.

ORIGIN

In 1966, social psychologist Elliot Aronson had participants listen to recordings of contestants (actors) answering questions on a radio game show. The contestants were either super smart, answering 92% of questions correctly, or not, answering only 30% correctly. In some tapes, the actors would spill coffee at the end of the interview. Aronson found that when the smart actor spilled coffee, he was rated as more attractive, but if the dumb-dumb spilled coffee, they hated his stupid face.

EXAMPLES

1. In spite of falling down at red carpets, Jennifer Lawrence is perceived as 'down-to-earth'. (excuse the pun)
2. When the Cybertruck window shattered during a presentation, Tesla made a T-shirt about it which helped secure 250k+ reservations in a week.
3. After a chicken shortage in 2018 led to temporary closures, KFC issued an apology with the headline "FCK", which the world thought was hilarious.

Video Examples

soundsm.art/pratfall

(For those of you that also have the audiobook, I apologize for the rant. lol)

Attribution Bias

We judge others' actions differently than our own.

ORIGIN

Attribution Bias was first explored in the 1970s by psychologists interested in understanding how we explain behavior. They observed that people tend to make different attributions (or explanations) for their own actions compared to others', often seeing their own actions as situational while attributing others' actions to personality or intent.

TYPES

1. **Fundamental Attribution Error:** If somebody cuts you off in traffic, you might assume they're a rude driver, rather than considering they might be in a rush due to an emergency or something.

2. **Actor-Observer Bias:** If you arrive late to work, you might blame traffic, but if somebody else is late, you might think they're garbage, they've always been garbage, and should get fired.

3. **Hostile Attribution Bias:** If somebody accidentally bumps into you, you take that shit personally.

4. **Self-Serving Bias:** See next page.

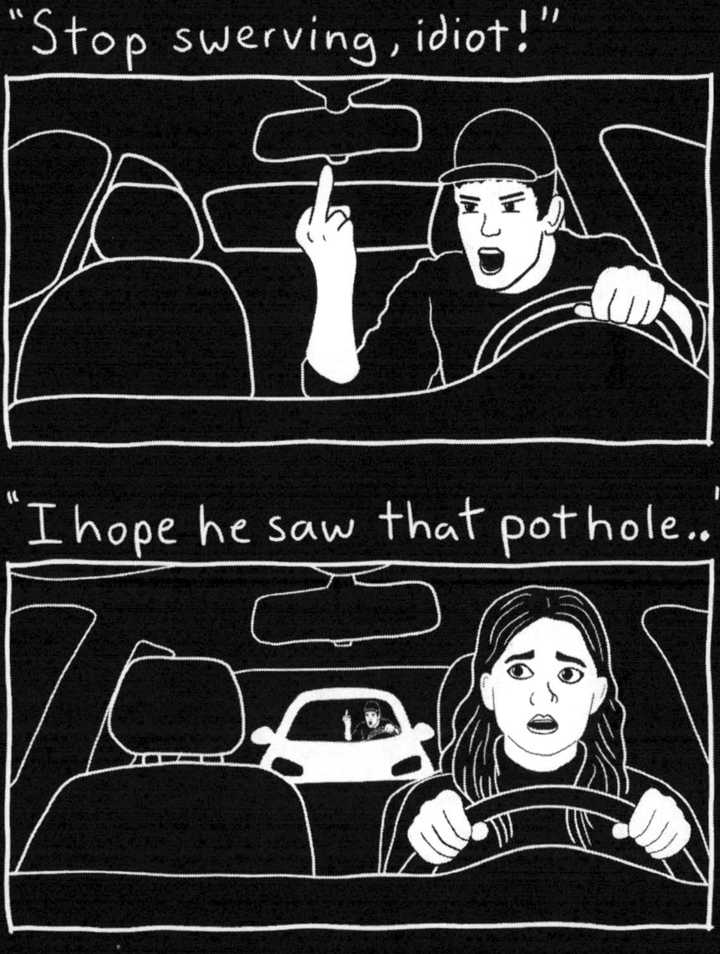
"Stop swerving, idiot!"
"I hope he saw that pot hole.."

Result

Good
Bad

Take Credit

Blame Others.

Self-Serving Bias

Taking credit for our successes but blaming our failures on external factors.

ORIGIN

Expanding on Attribution theory, Self-Serving Bias was introduced by Fritz Heider in 1958 as the idea that people tend to attribute their successes to internal factors while attributing failures to external factors.

EXAMPLES

1. **School** - Studies have shown that students often credit good grades to their intelligence and hard work, while attributing poor grades to external factors like unfair tests or poor teaching.

2. **Work** - Employees might credit their own discipline if rewarded for punctuality, but blame traffic or slow drivers if they are late to work.

3. **Content Creation** - YouTubers might attribute a video's view count to their own unique ideas but when videos don't perform as well, they claim to be 'shadowbanned'.

You ever notice how some soccer Moms will celebrate with their Kid after a win but scream at the coach after a loss? Yeah..

Availability Heuristic

We judge the likelihood of events based on how easily examples come to mind.

ORIGIN

In 1973, psychologists Amos Tversky and Daniel Kahneman asked participants to judge the frequency of certain causes of death. They found people assume dramatic causes of death happen more often than they actually do, while normal causes of death happen way less than they actually do, proving that events people can easily recall are assumed to happen more often.

EXAMPLES

Mainstream Media - Airplane crashes, shark attacks, and serial killings are all horrible ways to die, but they don't happen as often as one might think. They're just really easy to remember, especially when they're on the news every time they happen. If heart disease was dramatic and sudden, we'd be seeing that on the news too.

Creators - After noticing many creators "blowing up" overnight, smaller creators might assume that it happens more often than it actually does. Especially with an algorithm prioritizing what's popular. In reality, for every one creator that 'blows up,' hundreds of thousands of others remain small.

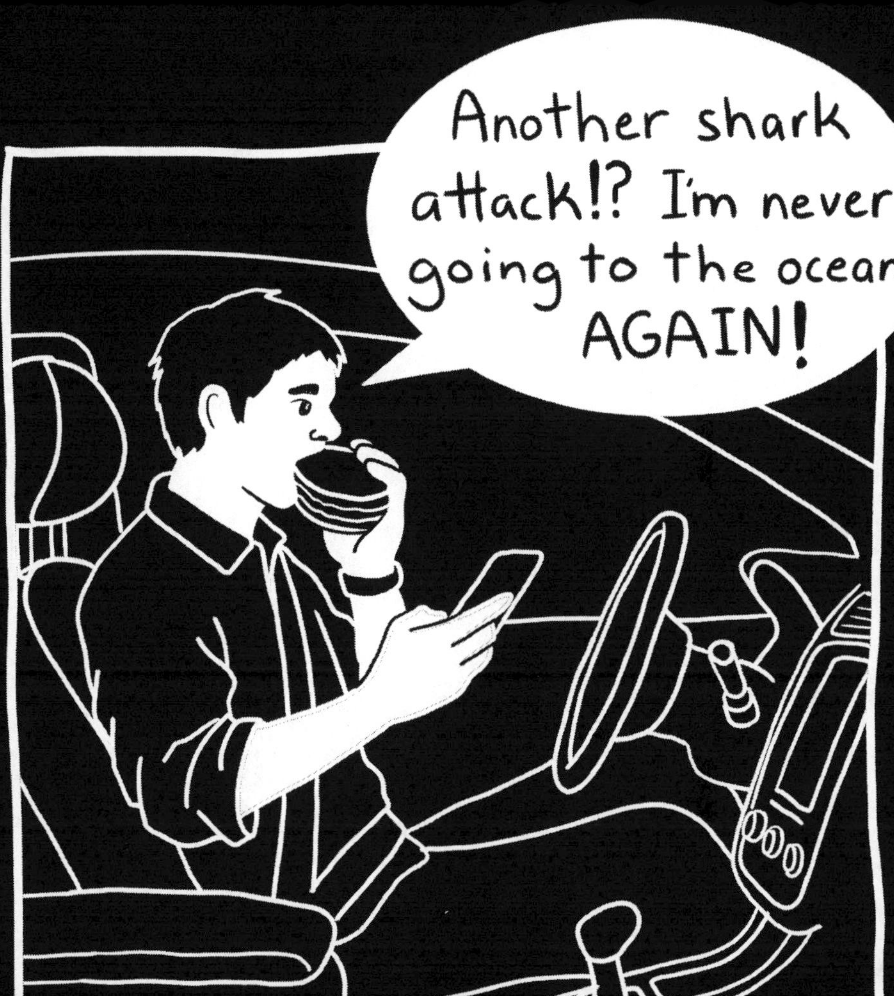
Another shark attack!? I'm never going to the ocean AGAIN!

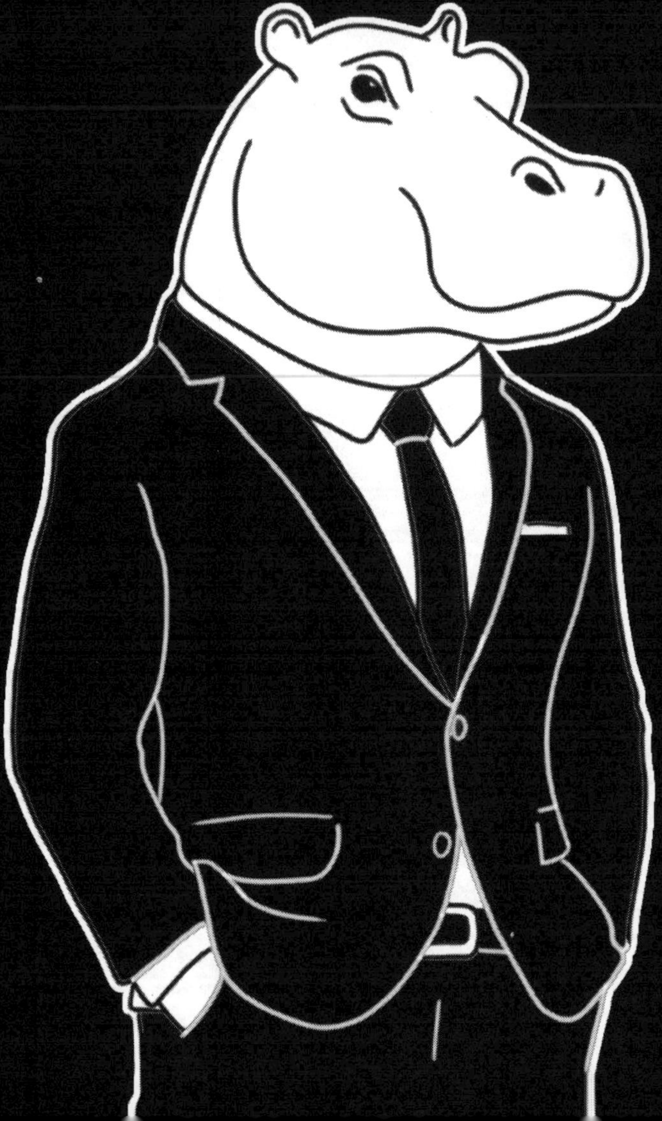

HiPPO Effect

The Highest Paid Person's Opinion often dominates decisions without data or insights.

ORIGIN

In his 2007 book, *Web Analytics: An Hour a Day*, author Avinash Kaushik describes how companies often rely on the "Highest Paid Person's Opinion" instead of data, leading to decisions that don't always benefit the user or the business.

EXAMPLES

- **Blockbuster:** When streaming was just starting, Blockbuster's leaders ignored the data and stuck to their traditional rental model, believing people would always prefer physical stores.

- **Nokia:** When smartphone technology was introduced to the mobile phone market, Nokia's leadership didn't take it seriously. They stuck with what worked, bricks you could use to call or text your friends. Anyone remember T9? God I'm old.

- **Kodak:** After inventing the first digital camera, Kodak's leadership decided to keep it under wraps out of fear it might hurt their film business. Their gatekeeping led to competitors dominating the market. You can't hold back technological advancement.

Focusing Effect

We place too much emphasis on one aspect of an event or decision, ignoring the rest.

ORIGIN

In 1998, psychologists David Schkade and Daniel Kahneman studied whether people believed Californians were happier than Midwesterners. Participants assumed Californians were happier due to the climate, however, actual happiness ratings showed no significant difference. This revealed that focusing on climate led to an overestimation of its impact on happiness.

In 2006, they also found that people overestimate the impact of income on happiness. While higher income can improve life satisfaction, its effect is less significant than one might expect. People tend to focus too much on finances and overlook other factors affecting well-being.

EXAMPLES

1. A person may choose a job based only on how much they'll make and not even consider things like distance or work-life balance.
2. When shopping for a new car, a buyer might focus on the appearance, or that $2K was knocked off the asking price instead of focusing on its mileage, how good it is on gas, or even if it's bullet proof.

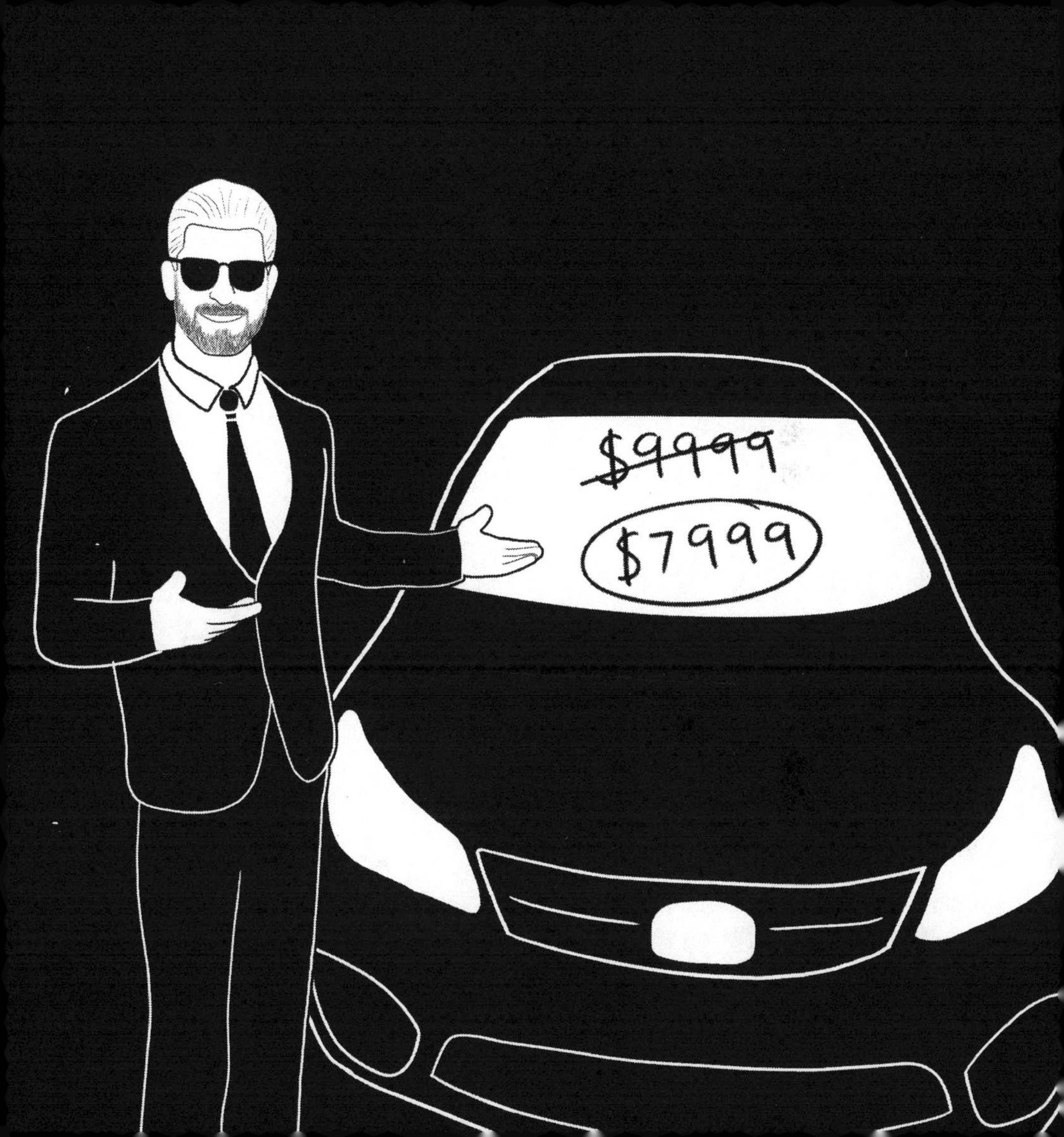

$9999
$7999

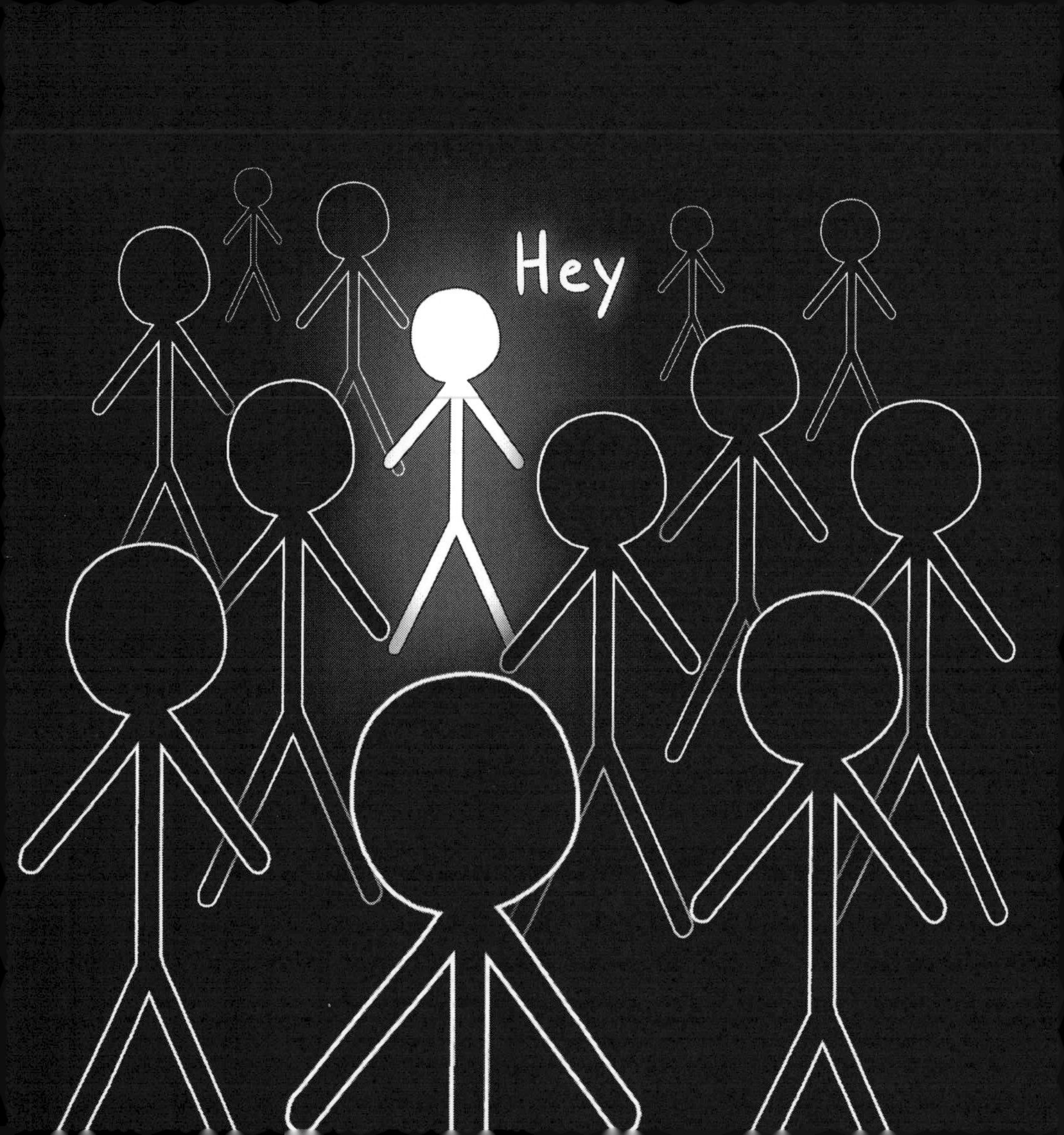
Hey

Cocktail Party Effect

(Selective Attention)

The ability to hear one voice among many

ORIGIN

In 1953, cognitive scientist Colin Cherry conducted an experiment where participants wore headphones and listened to two overlapping voices, one in each ear. He found that people could focus on one conversation and tune out the other, but they'd immediately notice if their name was said, even from the ignored voice.

Worst. ASMR. Ever.

MAIN EXAMPLE

Ever been at a loud party, when you suddenly hear your name from across the room? That selective attention is the Cocktail Party Effect. Your brain tunes out background noise as it detects something personally relevant.

OTHER EXAMPLES

1. Hearing your phone ring at a concert.
2. Hearing an announcement in a busy train station.
3. Talking on the phone in a noisy city.

Region-Beta Paradox

People can sometimes be better off in worse situations.

IMAGINE THIS:

You just moved closer to your workplace, but you don't know exactly how far away it is from your house. Before finding out, you decide that if your office is less than a mile away, you'll walk to work, but if it's more than a mile away, you'll drive. Now.. if your office is 2 miles away.. funny enough, you'll end up getting to work faster than if it were 1 mile away.

The worse situation (your office being further away) ended up being better for you (get there faster) because it forced you to find a solution (drive).

Intense discomfort triggers us to find immediate solutions while mild discomfort is easier to put up with leading to a prolonged experience of it.

OTHER EXAMPLES:

- **Work:** An unpleasant job might annoy someone for years but a super shitty job would have that person updating their resume immediately.
- **Relationships:** A boring relationship is endurable, but an exhausting relationship is a deal breaker.

"Comfort is the enemy of progress"
- P.T. Barnum (pg. 32)

HIGH

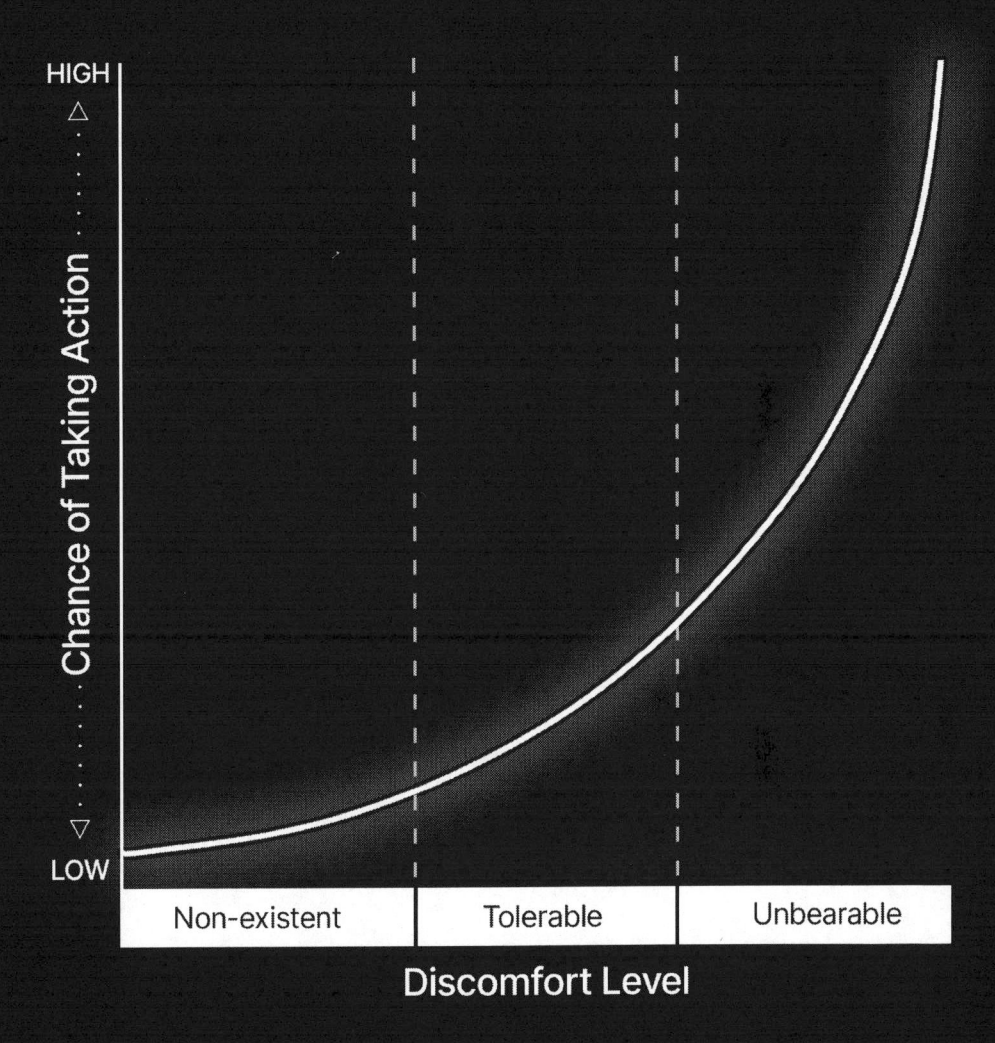

Chance of Taking Action

LOW

Non-existent | Tolerable | Unbearable

Discomfort Level

Nice typo, idoit!

Muphry's Law

***When you correct someone else's writing,
you're likely to make a mistake yourself.***

ORIGIN

You read that right. MU*PHR*Y. Not Murphy. In a 1992 newsletter, editor John Bangsund coined the term "Muphry's Law", a deliberate misspelling of "Murphy's Law," highlighting the irony that critiques of writing often include mistakes.

*Bagsund's article, 1992
(image)*

soundsm.art/muphryslaw

HILARIOUS EXAMPLE

In 2009, the British Prime Minister hand-wrote a letter to a mourning mother who lost her son in Afghanistan, but he misspelled the man's last name. The Sun (newspaper) criticized him publicly but they ALSO misspelled the man's last name, forcing them to publish an apology. lol

MUPHRY'S LAW (FULL VERSION)

1. If you write a critique of someone else's writing, there will be a mistake of some kind in what you have written.
2. If an author thanks you in a book for your editing or proofreading, there will be mistakes in the book.
3. The stronger the sentiment expressed in 1 and 2, the greater the fault.
4. Any book devoted to editing or style will be internally inconsistent.

Semantic Satiation

Repeating a word so many times that it temporarily loses its meaning.

ORIGIN

In his 1962 experiment, Leon Jakobovits James found that when participants repeated words out loud they struggled with cognitive tasks related to those words.

So basically, when the part of the brain that says the word has neural activity firing over and over, it reacts by chilling the f*** out. So basically, that part of the brain goes into dumb mode for a moment.

STORYTIME

So there my Mom was walking into the kitchen to get a late night snack. Suddenly she stops, stares straight ahead, and will not take another step. She was frozen out of fear, because across the kitchen she saw the silhouette of a man sitting at the kitchen table. So there she is, standing as still as possible when she starts to hear this faint whispering..

"Gravy.. Gravy... Gravy.."

It was me. I was eating my own late night snack (mashed potatoes) when suddenly the word 'gravy' lost all meaning.

Gravy
Gravy
Gravy
Gravy
Gravy
Gravy
Gravy
Gravy
Gravy
Gravy
Gravy
Gravy
Gravy
Gravy
Gravy
Gravy
Gravy
Gravy
Gravy
Gravy

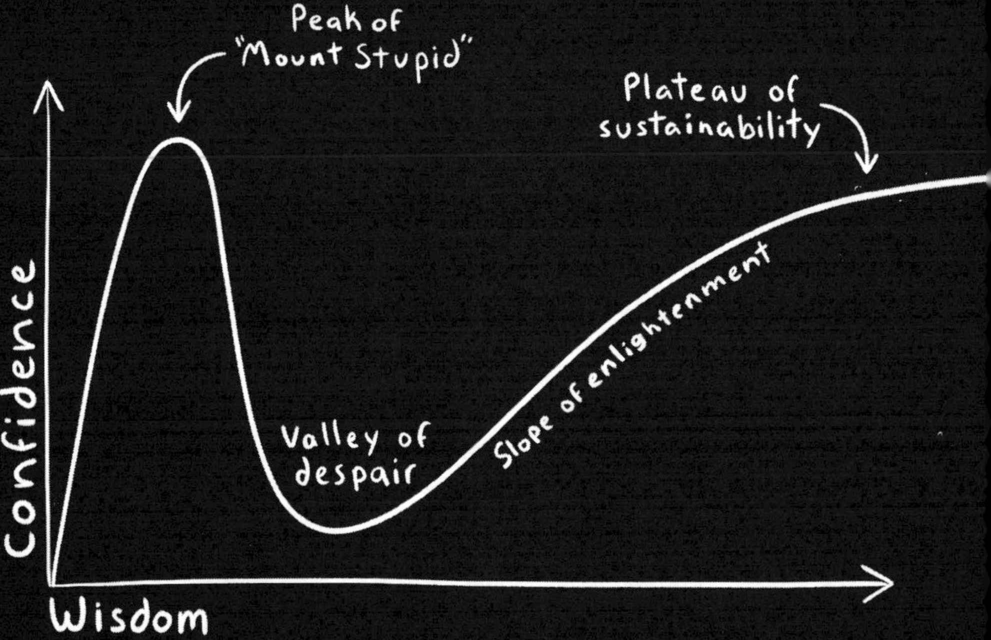
Peak of
"Mount Stupid"
Plateau of
sustainability
Confidence
Valley of
despair
Slope of enlightenment
Wisdom

Dunning-Kruger Effect

***Novices overestimate their competence,
while experts underestimate theirs.***

ORIGIN

In 1999, psychologists David Dunning and Justin Kruger conducted experiments to measure people's self-assessment of skills in areas like grammar, logic, and humor. They found that participants who believed they tested better than 62% of their peers actually scored in the bottom 12%.

EXAMPLES

1. Low-performing students often exhibit overconfidence in their abilities, which can hinder their learning and performance.

2. Individuals with limited knowledge about political issues may perceive themselves as more knowledgeable than they are. (We all know that guy)

3. People who lack self-awareness regarding their competencies may contribute to poor decision-making in teams.

Pro Tip (Creators): Have you ever heard the term 'Loud Minority'? Well.. When it comes to negative comments, the Dunning-Kruger Effect kind of explains it. For every hater on the internet chillin on Mt. Stupid, passing out dumb comments like candy, there are 100 others that want to positively engage with your content, but don't think they're qualified to do so.

Goal Gradient Effect

The closer we get to a goal, the faster we work to achieve it.

ORIGIN

In 1932, behaviorist Clark L. Hull observed that rats in a maze would run faster as they approached a food reward, suggesting that the animals' motivation intensified with proximity to the goal.

EXAMPLES

- **Consumerism:** Psychologists Kivetz, Urminsky, and Zheng (2006) found that customers with nearly completed punch cards in loyalty programs tend to buy more frequently to earn rewards sooner.

- **Charity:** Studies show that people are more likely to donate to campaigns nearing their fundraising targets, as the close goal boosts their motivation to contribute.

- **Creators:** I was recently in a 2 Million Subscriber livestream and as I was talking to chat, viewers suddenly just started flooding in. The hours leading up to that moment, the sub count grew somewhat slowly. But as soon as it hit 1,999,900, it only took a few minutes to hit 2 Million. *That* is the Goal Gradient Effect.

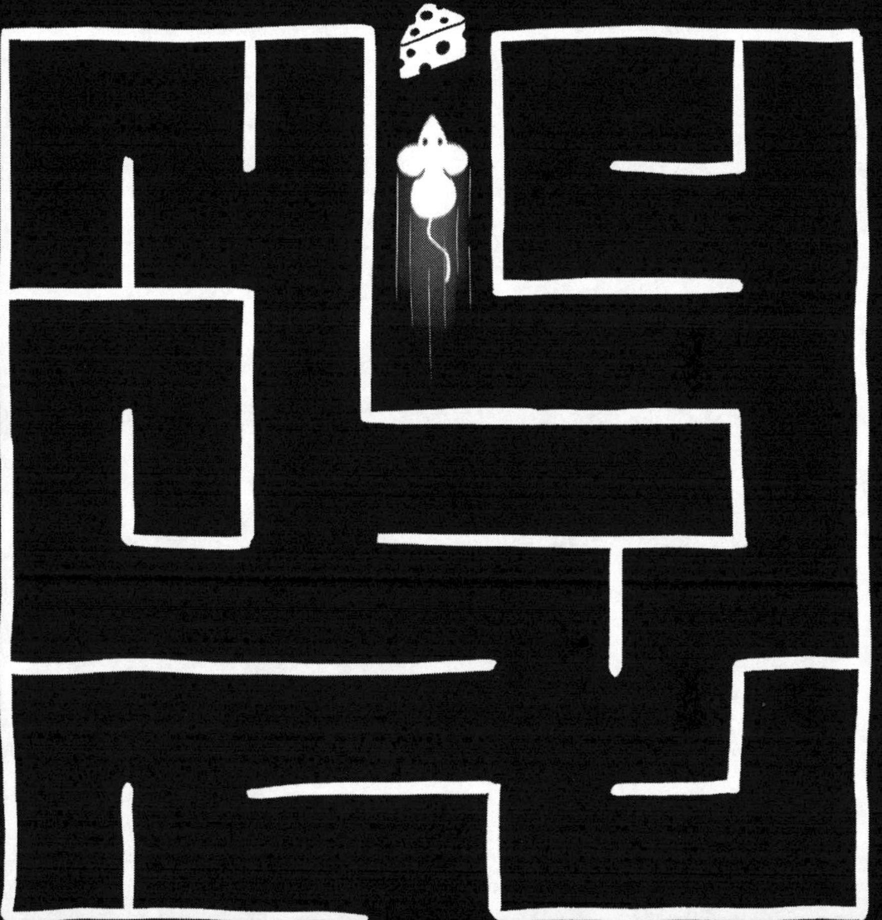

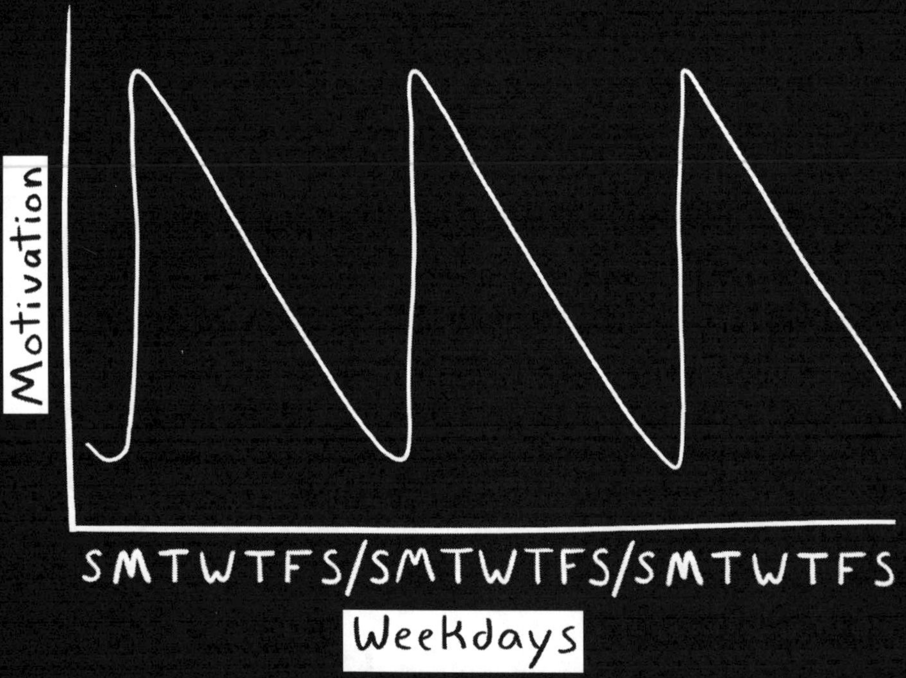
Motivation
SMTWTFS/SMTWTFS/SMTWTFS
Weekdays

Fresh Start Effect

People are more motivated to pursue goals after a major life event or temporal milestone, like a birthday or New Year.

ORIGIN

In 2014, researchers found that people are more likely to start positive behaviors, like exercising or dieting, at the beginning of new time periods, like a new year, month, or week.

By examining google search trends or gym attendance records, you can see the 'fresh start' data for yourself.

EXAMPLES

1. **New Year's Resolutions:** Starting January 1st, I'm jogging every day!
2. **'Start on Monday' Mentality:** After this weekend, I'm done with sweets.
3. **Birthday Resolutions:** I'm 30 now, I better stop wasting money if I ever want to have my own house.

Fun Fact - New research indicates that the Fresh Start Effect works best when a person experiences failure right before the restart. If the person is on track to achieving their goals and they do a 'fresh start' to improve even more, it can backfire and they can lose their momentum completely.

Sampling Bias

Drawing conclusions from an unrepresentative sample, leading to skewed results.

TYPES

1. **Undercoverage Bias:** Occurs when certain members of a population are underrepresented. *Example:* A survey conducted via landline phones might miss individuals who primarily use mobile phones.

2. **Self-Selection Bias:** Happens when individuals choose to participate, skewing the sample. *Example:* Online polls often over-represent people with strong opinions, as they're more likely to respond.

3. **Survivorship Bias:** Involves focusing on subjects that passed a selection process, overlooking those that didn't. *Example:* Analyzing successful companies without including failed ones can skew insights into business success.

Other Types

Pro-Tip (Creators): Remember the 'Loud Minority' on the Dunning-Kruger Effect page? A small sample of people with strong opinions get 'represented' by filling up the comments while the quiet majority prefers to stay silent. If engagement continues to grow, people like it, even if there aren't many that voice it.

soundsm.art/samplingbias

"Algorithm know, thats why it grow." - John Scott

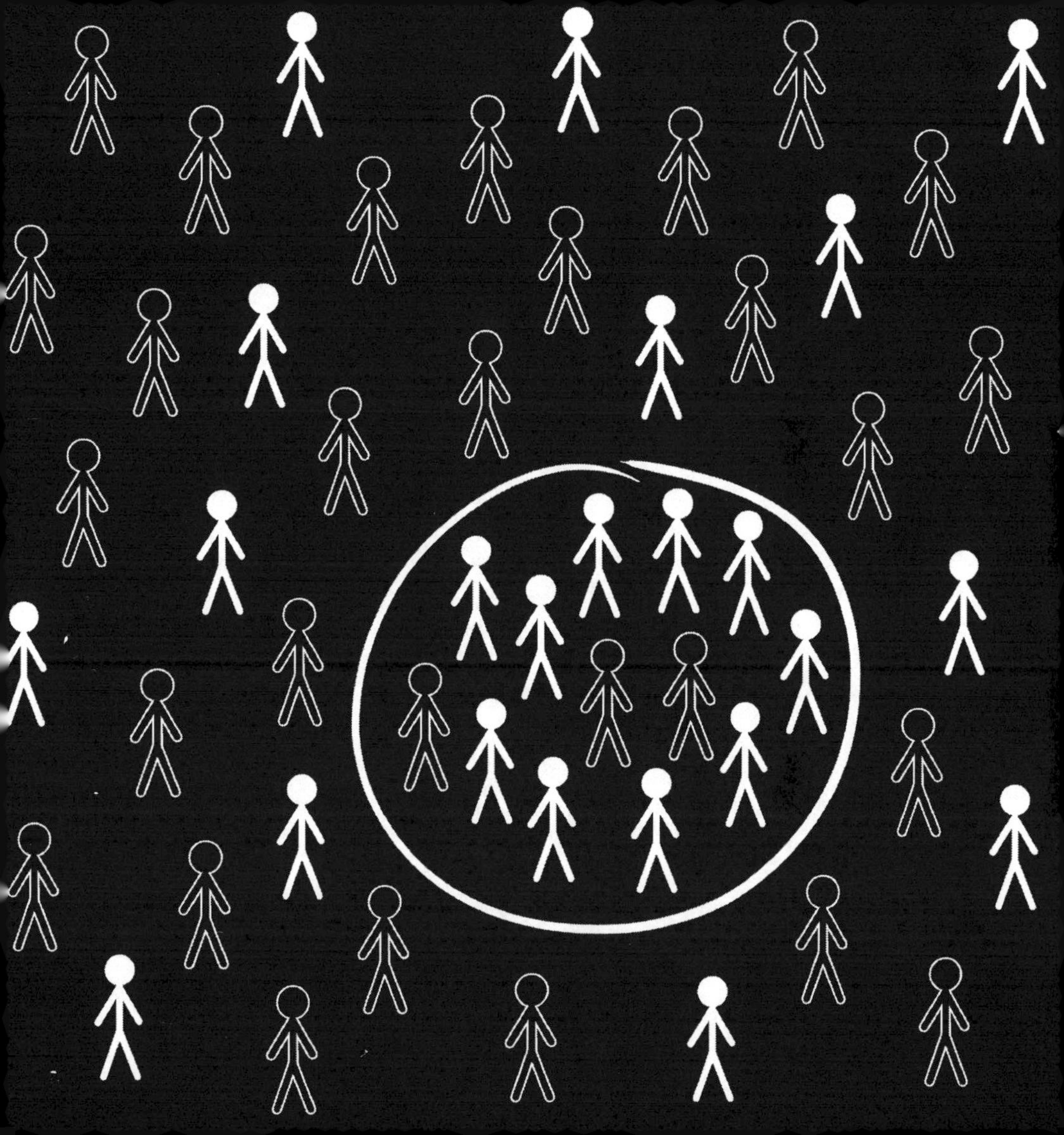

Social Loafing

People tend to put in less effort when working in groups than when working alone.

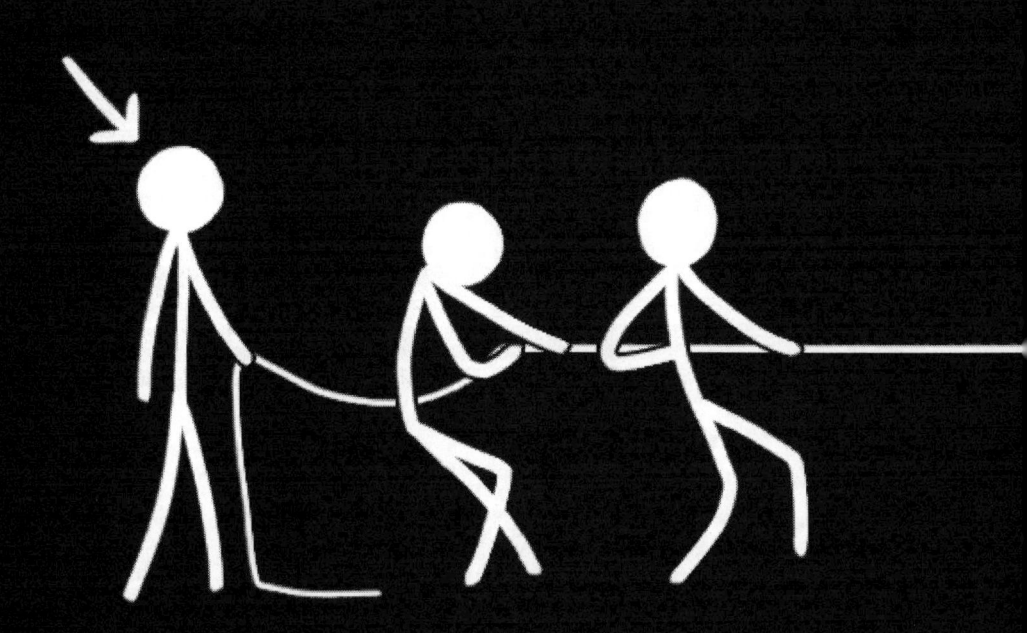

SO THIS IS KINDA INTERESTING:

In a 1979 study, participants were asked to shout and clap as loudly as possible. When individuals performed alone, they gave maximum effort but when they believed they were part of a group (even when they weren't), their individual effort decreased by about 60% in groups of six. Something I never really thought about until now but I would definitely have clapped less enthusiastically as well.

~~FIRST~~ Only IDEA

Einstellung Effect

When your existing knowledge blocks you from seeing a better solution.

ORIGIN

In 1942, psychologists Abraham S. Luchins and Edith Hirsch Luchins ran their famous water jar experiment in which participants were tasked with measuring specific amounts of water using three jars of varying capacities.

TASK EXAMPLE

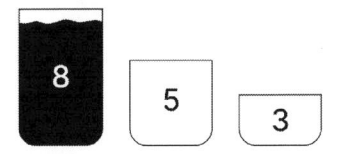

Move the water so that the first and second jugs both contain 4 units, and the third is empty.

The participants did several of these tasks and eventually when an easier task came along they applied the more difficult solution even when there was an easier and much quicker way to solve it.

SOFTWARE

If you're anything like me, you often figure things out by experimenting, but being self-taught can mean you end up taking the long way around for years until a 5-minute tutorial makes you realize how much time you've wasted.

Curse of Knowledge

Incorrectly assuming that everyone knows as much as you do on a given topic.

ORIGIN

In 1989, economists Colin Camerer, George Loewenstein, and Martin Weber did extensive research on decision-making. They concluded that better-informed individuals often fail to account for the knowledge gaps of others.

When you have advanced knowledge on a subject, it makes it difficult to explain that knowledge to somebody who doesn't. This is exactly why learning something new can be so intimidating sometimes.. You enter that world and immediately feel like you're behind.

EXAMPLES

1. A YouTuber trying to explain something simple with terms like 'CTR' 'AVD' 'RPM' 'CPM' etc..
2. A creator posting an image with an inside joke they assume their audience already knows.

Try this - Think of a popular song, tap it out on a table with your fingers and have someone try to guess what song it is. To you, it will be so obvious it might actually annoy you when the person can't figure it out.

How you think it be

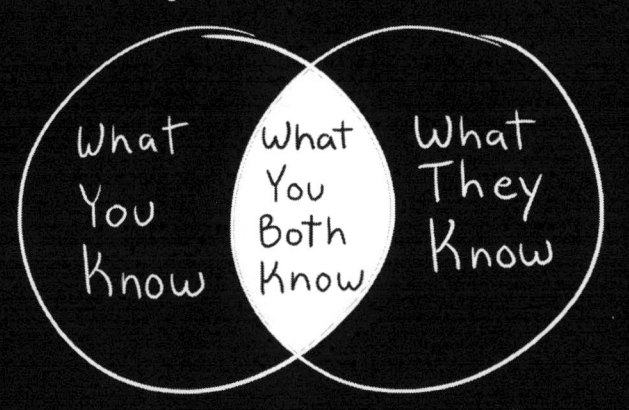

- What You Know
- What You Both Know
- What They Know

How it really be

- What You Know
- "The F*** Are You Talkin About?"

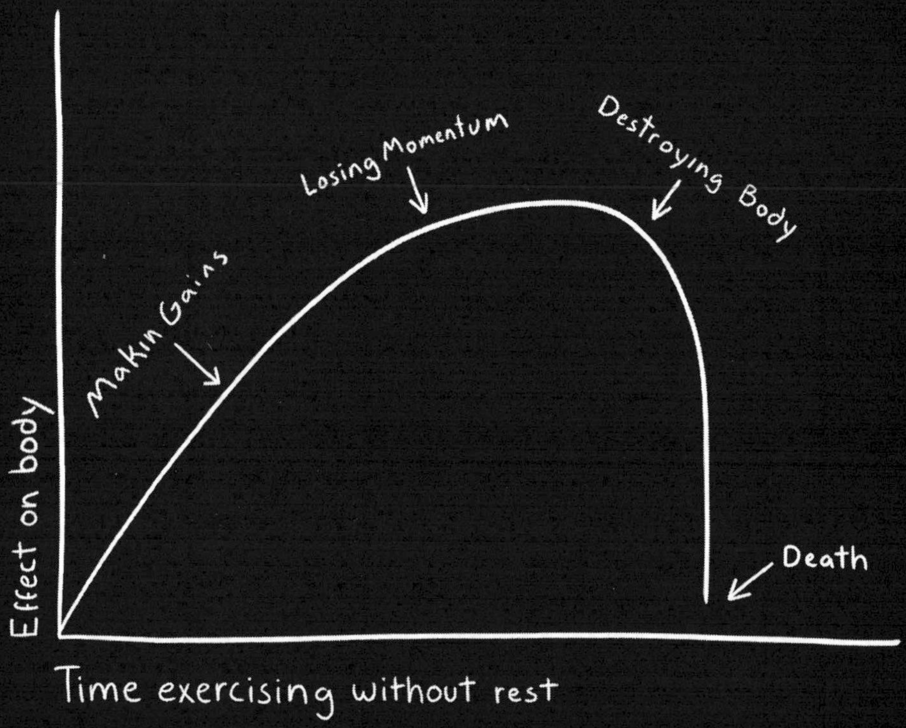
Effect on body
Makin Gains
Losing Momentum
Destroying Body
Death
Time exercising without rest

Law of Diminishing Returns

The more effort you invest,
the smaller the returns become.

ORIGIN

In the early 19th century, after the war in England, rising costs of growing crops led farmers to dedicate more labor to farming. They noticed that as they added more workers to the same land, the extra harvest from each new worker began to shrink. So put simply:

At first: Each additional worker can help maximize the use of the land.
But eventually: The land is almost fully used, and with each additional worker, the less space and resources they have to work with.

OTHER EXAMPLES

Gains: Pushing hard at the gym initially boosts fitness gains, but without rest, each additional workout yields less benefit until fatigue, injury, or burnout eventually halt progress entirely.

Studying: In the first hour, understanding and retention improve. In the second hour, concentration starts fading. Each additional hour provides less benefit until mental exhaustion slows progress.

Diminishing Returns of Content Creation

soundsm.art/lodr

Isolation Effect

Things that stand out are more memorable than things that blend in.

ORIGIN

In her 1933 study, psychiatrist Hedwig von Restorff presented participants with lists of items where one item was notably different in some way—such as color, size, or category. She discovered that these distinctive items were more likely to be recalled than the others. She also did this with letters, numbers, shapes, etc.. and the results were the same.

EXAMPLES:

1. **Marketing:** Brands use bright colors or unique packaging to make products stand out on shelves.//
2. **User Interface Design:** Designers use contrasting colors or unique icons to draw attention to important features or calls to action, improving user experience and engagement. Especially when it's paired with Fitts' Law. Remember that? (Pg. 12)

Cool Fact: Many years later (2011), research showed that neighboring items were also recalled fairly easily.. So whatever you really REALLY need to remember.. Pair it with something that sticks out.

SOUP

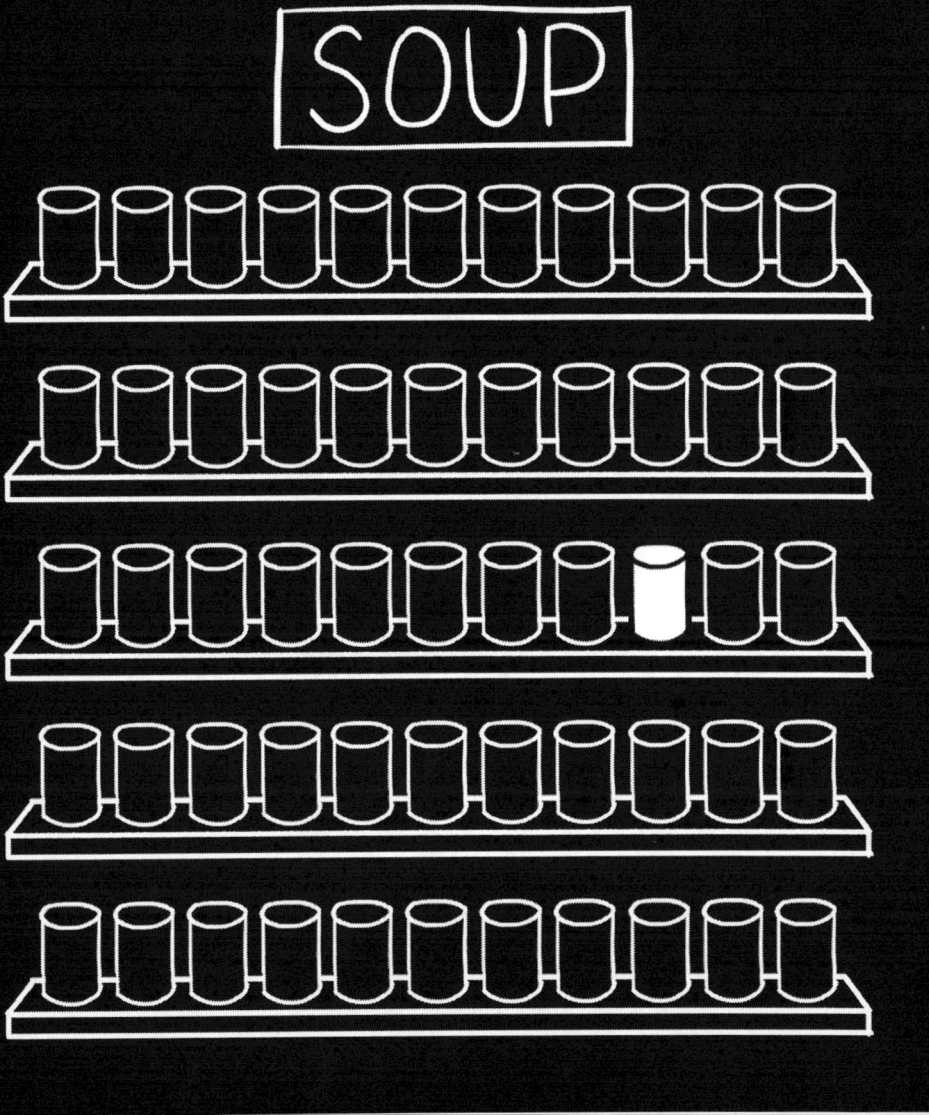

Sir! We've finally discovered a cure for cancer!
What!? Let me see that!
BIG PHARMA
No one can ever know about this..

Shirky Principle

When problems are preserved by those meant to solve them.

ORIGIN

In 2010, writer and social media theorist Clay Shirky observed that institutions often act to preserve the problems they are meant to address. This insight was highlighted by author Kevin Kelly, who named it the "Shirky Principle."

EXAMPLES

- **Healthcare:** Medical organizations may focus on treating symptoms rather than curing diseases, ensuring a continuous need for their services.
- **Charities:** Some charities might prioritize maintaining their operations over effectively solving the issues they address, to justify their ongoing existence.
- **Mechanic:** Temporary fixes = job security. Permanent repairs = less future work.

Note about A.I. - Like I wrote on page 47, you can't hold back technological advancement. Imagine if tractors were never invented because farmers didn't want to lose their jobs. People may fear A.I. will replace them and some might try to preserve some problems it can easily fix, but A.I. won't replace the value of human attention; it will free it up from lower-value tasks.

Bystander Effect

The more people in the area of an emergency, the less likely any will help.

ORIGIN

In 1964, a 28-year-old bartender was stabbed to death in Queens, N.Y. while 38 witnesses failed to intervene. Some say that number is bullshit, and the story is exaggerated.. Whatever.. the important part is that it inspired the research of why people are less likely to help when others are present.

In 1968, psychologists John Darley and Bibb Latané conducted an experiment where people overheard someone pretending to have a seizure. They found that people choose to help more when they are alone, but are less likely to help as the number of bystanders increased.

REASONS

1. They feel less responsible with others around.
2. People monitor others around them to determine how to act.
3. Fear of judgment or embarrassment.

Whether it's witnessing a medical emergency, someone being bullied, or just some dude being an asshole on the subway, The Bystander Effect can really make humans seem.. inhumane.

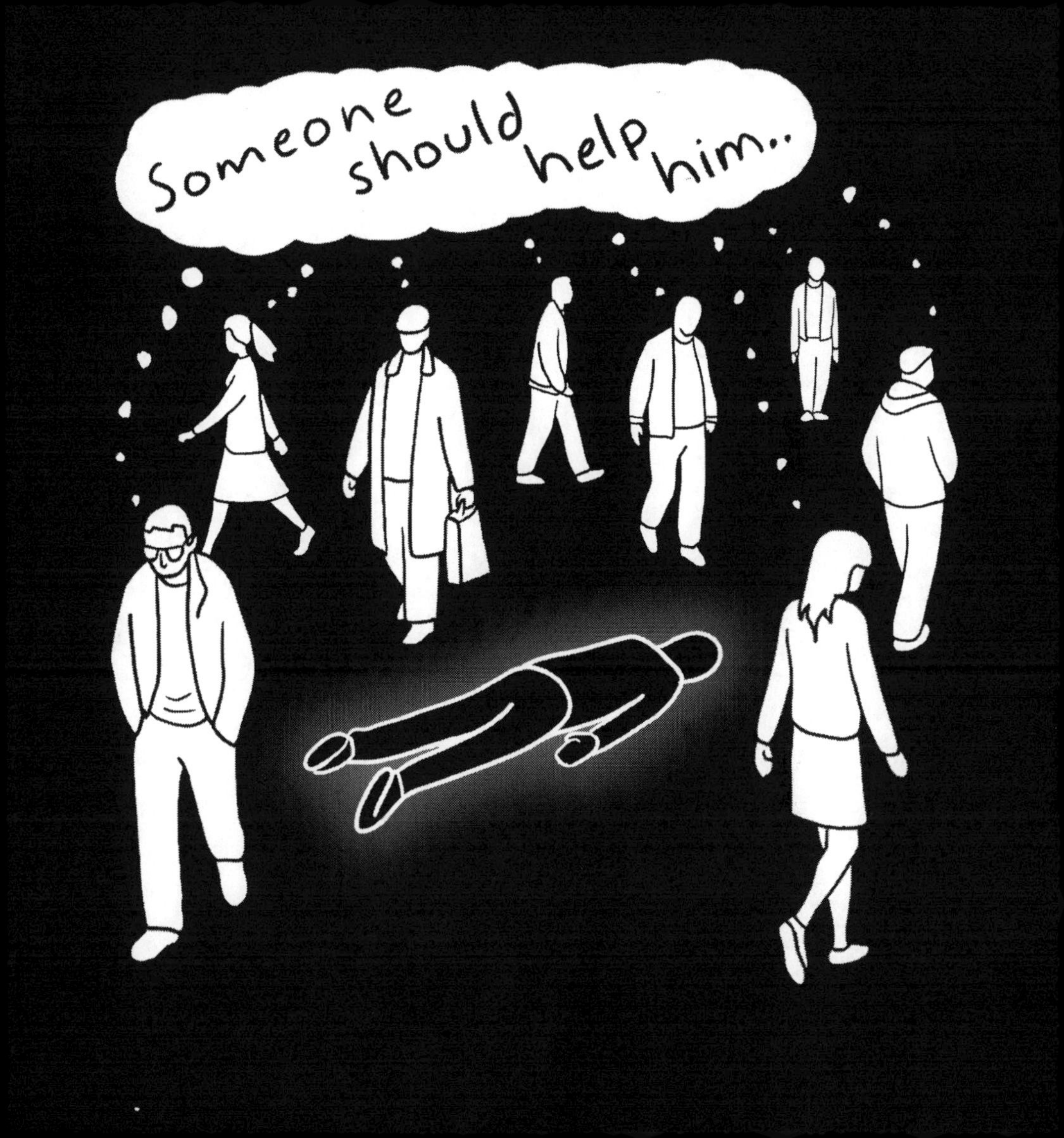
Someone should help him..

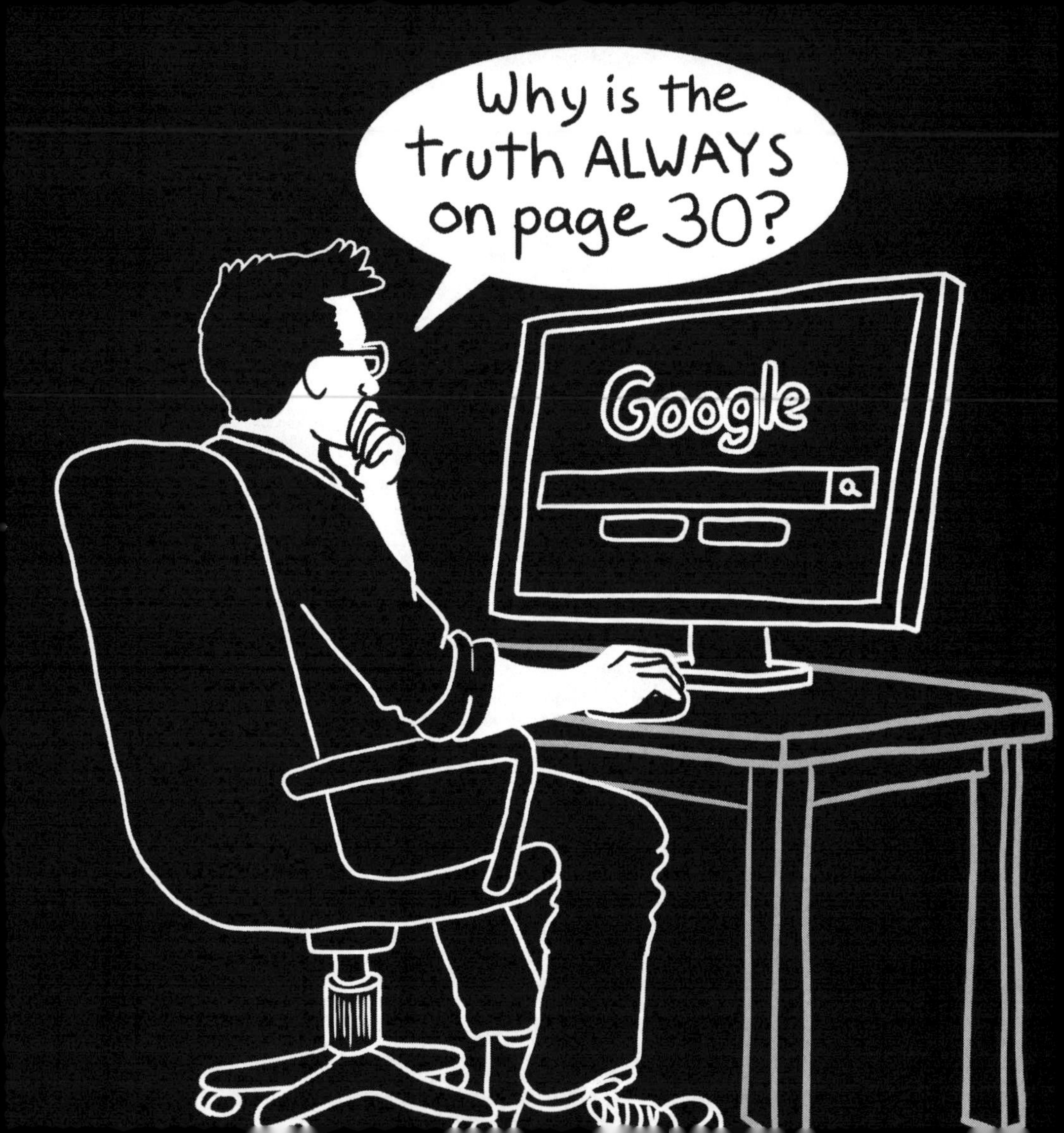
Why is the truth ALWAYS on page 30?
Google

Confirmation Bias

Seeking out and favoring information that confirms existing beliefs.

ORIGIN

In the 17th century book Novum Organum (Yeah we goin way back) philosopher Fancis Bacon wrote about how people tend to interpret information in a way that supports their existing opinions. 400 years later, psychologist Peter Wason conducted experiments to confirm the idea.

EXAMPLES

Medical: Doctors may favor information that supports their initial diagnosis, potentially overlooking contradictory evidence.

Legal: Police, judges or juries may only consider evidence that aligns with preexisting beliefs, ignoring other (possibly important) details.

Scientific Research: Researchers may design experiments or interpret data in ways that confirm their hypotheses, potentially leading to biased conclusions.

Media Consumption: Individuals often select news sources that align with their political beliefs.

Personal Relationships: Someone who believes a colleague is unfriendly may interpret neutral behaviors as negative. (*Hostile Attribution Bias* Pg. 40)

Imposter Syndrome

Feeling like a fraud, even when you're skilled and accomplished.

ORIGIN

In 1978, psychologists Pauline Clance and Suzanne Imes first described Imposter Syndrome after studying high-achieving individuals who felt undeserving of their success. This phenomenon has since been recognized as a common experience among professionals across all fields.

EXAMPLES

Professionals: A newly promoted manager may feel unqualified for their role, attributing their advancement to luck rather than merit, and fear being exposed as incompetent.

Students: A student who excels academically might believe their success is due to external factors, such as easy exams, rather than their intelligence and hard work.

Content Creators: A creator can easily brush off viral video like it was luck, stating that 'It was just good timing' or they 'jumped on a trend'..

I know this, because I've been that creator.

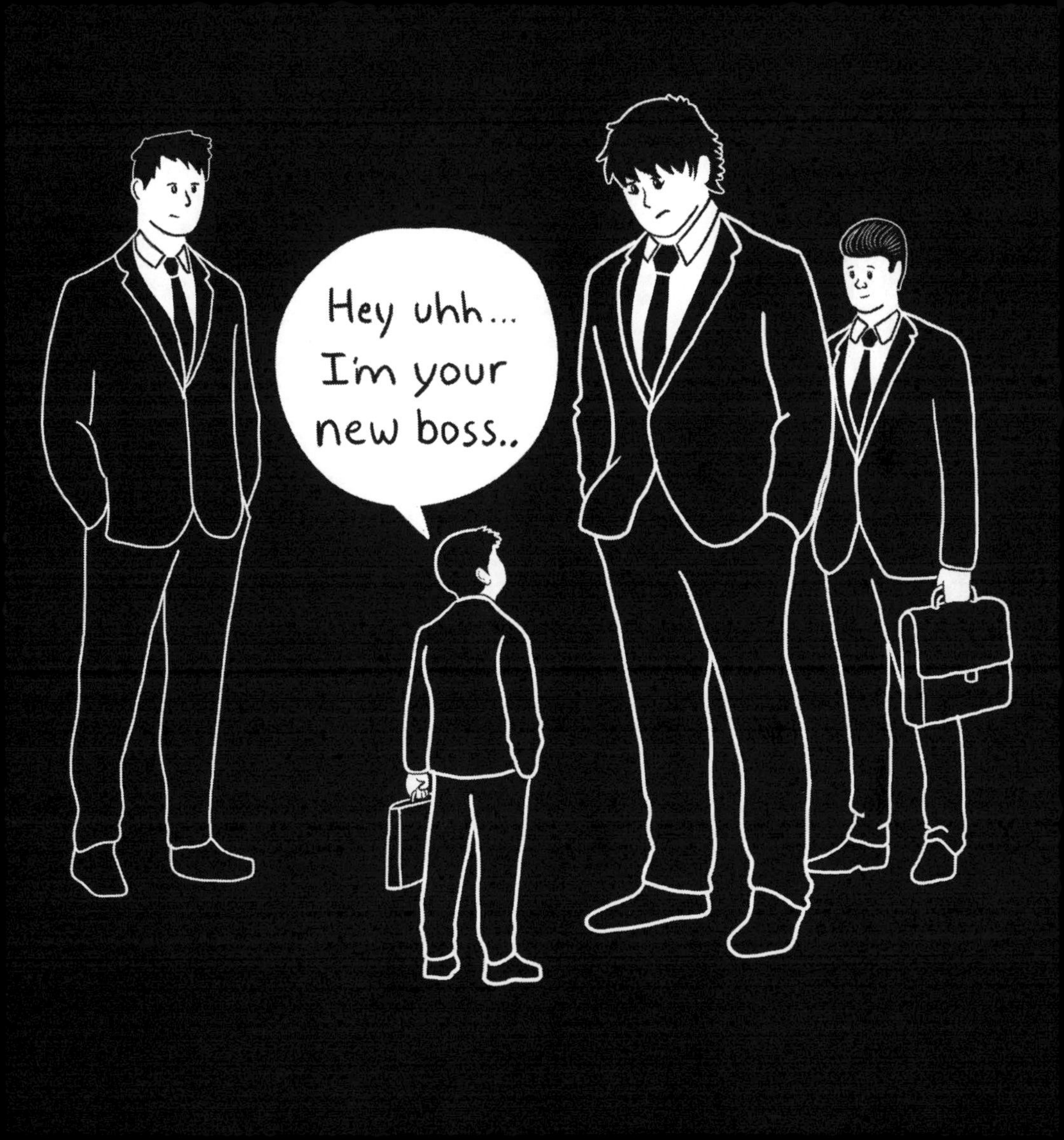
Hey uhh...
I'm your
new boss..

I can't quit!
I spent way too much time and effort getting this job!

Sunk Cost Fallacy

We keep investing in something just because we've already put time or money into it.

AUTHOR RANT:

Have you ever worked on a personal project for so long that, by the end, you hated it? You might have finished it only because you didn't want all that effort to go to waste. That's 'Sunk Cost' and it fucking sucks..

Pro Tip (Personal Projects): Never finish a personal project because you feel like you HAVE to.. If you ain't feelin it.. You've got two choices.

1. Stop. Save yourself the time, keep your sanity intact, and move on to something that actually excites you.. **OR..**
2. Finish it and feel like you've wasted even MORE time..

It's tough to get out of this trap when we're in it.. But I mean.. What do we think is gonna happen? We're going to magically love it once it's finished?

P.S. I first learned about this from *Better Call Saul.* Bravo Vince.

Abilene Paradox

When a group makes a decision that no one in the group actually wants.

ORIGIN

In a 1974 article, management expert Jerry B. Harvey tells the story of when his family drove 50 miles to Abilene, Texas on a hot, miserable, summer day. Thing was, none of them actually wanted to go. Each of them just assumed the others were excited about it.

Why though? Well, here's what Jerry said.

REASONS

Action Anxiety: Fear of negative consequences for voicing true opinions.
Negative Fantasies: Imagining adverse outcomes from expressing dissent.
Real Risk: Actual potential for negative repercussions.
Fear of Separation: Concern about being ostracized for disagreeing.

When I first heard of this I'm like "Isn't that just groupthink?"

NOPE.

With *groupthink*, everyone is on board because they don't want to be the only one that isn't. The *Abilene Paradox*, however, is THINKING everyone is on board, when no one really is.

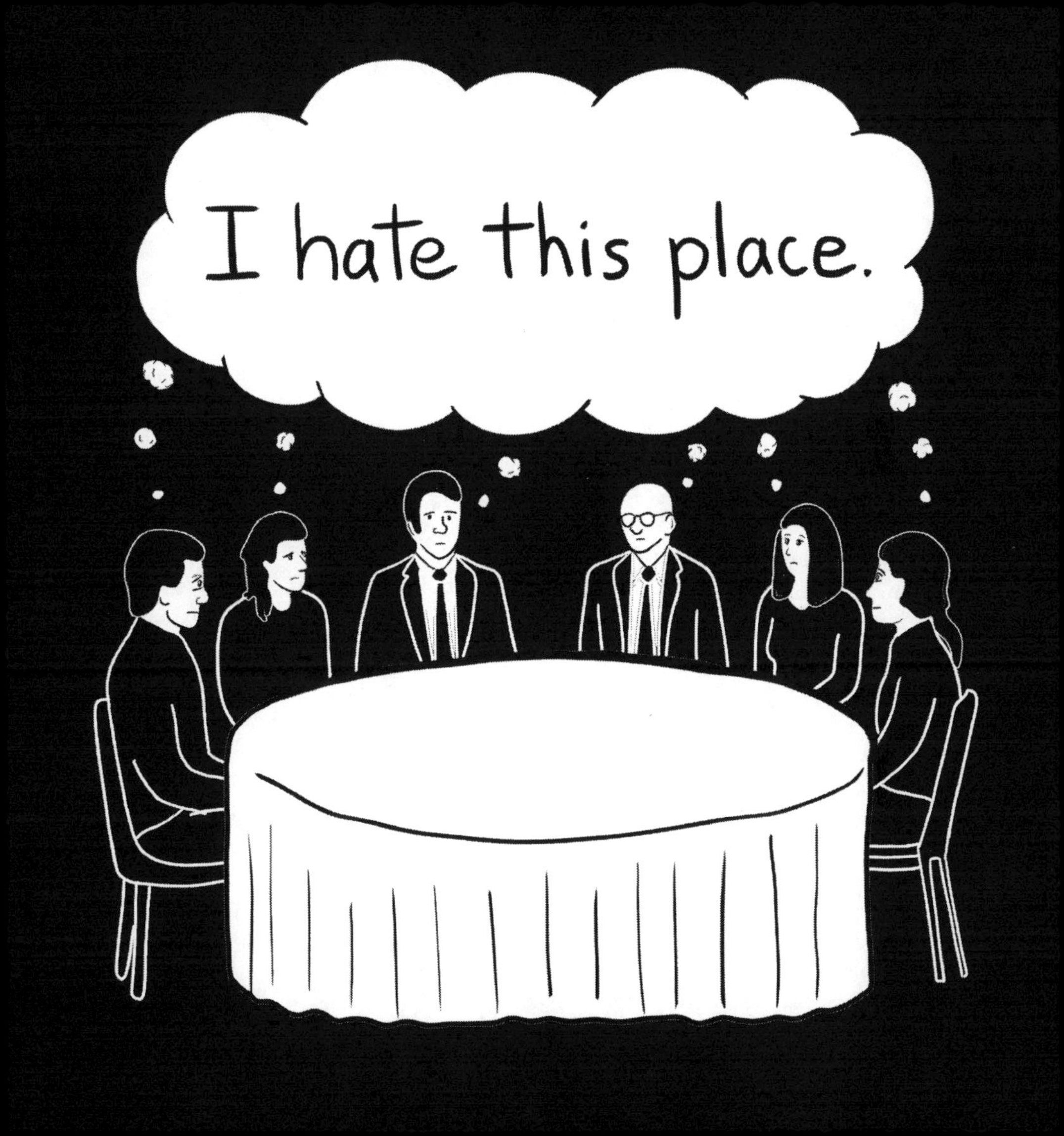
I hate this place.

noitall

The Earth is absolutely flat.

⬆ 19 ⬇ 💬 Reply Share

> **brandolini**
>
> That's just not true.
>
> ⬆ 1 ⬇ 💬 Reply Share
>
> > **noitall**
> >
> > You got proof?
> >
> > ⬆ 10 ⬇ 💬 Reply Share
> >
> > > **brandolini**
> > >
> > > I had a free hour. Here's all the research.
> > >
> > > [Link#1](#), [Link#2](#), [Link#3](#), [Link#4](#)
> > >
> > > ⬆ 1 ⬇ 💬 Reply Share
> > >
> > > > **noitall**
> > > >
> > > > Yea.. no. That's all fake
> > > >
> > > > ⬆ 9 ⬇ 💬 Reply Share

Brandolini's Law

It takes significantly more effort to refute false information than to produce it.

ORIGIN

In 2013, programmer Alberto Brandolini observed how easy it is for misinformation to spread and the difficulty of debunking it. He tweeted: "The amount of energy needed to refute bullshit is an order of magnitude bigger than to produce it."
And so it's commonly called the "Bullshit Asymmetry Principle"

EXAMPLES

- After the Boston Marathon bombing, a rumor spread on social media that a student who survived the Sandy Hook shooting had been killed in the bombing. Despite efforts to debunk it, including a Snopes investigation, the false story was shared over 92,000 times and covered by major news outlets.

- The false claim that vaccines cause autism persists today despite decades of research disproving it, continuing to harm public health through vaccine avoidance.

Relevant Adage: "A lie can travel halfway around the world before the truth can get its boots on"

Chesterton's Fence

Before removing a rule or system, understand why it was put there first.

ORIGIN

In his 1929 book, writer G.K. Chesterton emphasizes the importance of understanding an existing rule or law before changing or removing it. He said that if you come across a fence in a field and don't see its purpose, you shouldn't tear it down until you understand why it was built.

EXAMPLES

Urban Planning: Existing infrastructure elements like pedestrian zones may seem outdated but understanding its original intent, like reducing traffic, might prevent a major traffic jam.

Policy Making: Before repealing a regulation, learning why it exists might prevent reviving the issues.

Warehouse Safety: In the tv show *The Office*, The employees attend a safety meeting in the warehouse. *Rule: Only qualified operators can use the forklift.* Michael Scott (not qualified) argues and eventually breaks that rule. He then knocks down all of the warehouse shelves and Chesteron's Fence with it.

Michael Scott wrecks the forklift

soundsm.art/michaelscott

I hate this fence.
I'm gonna knock it down.

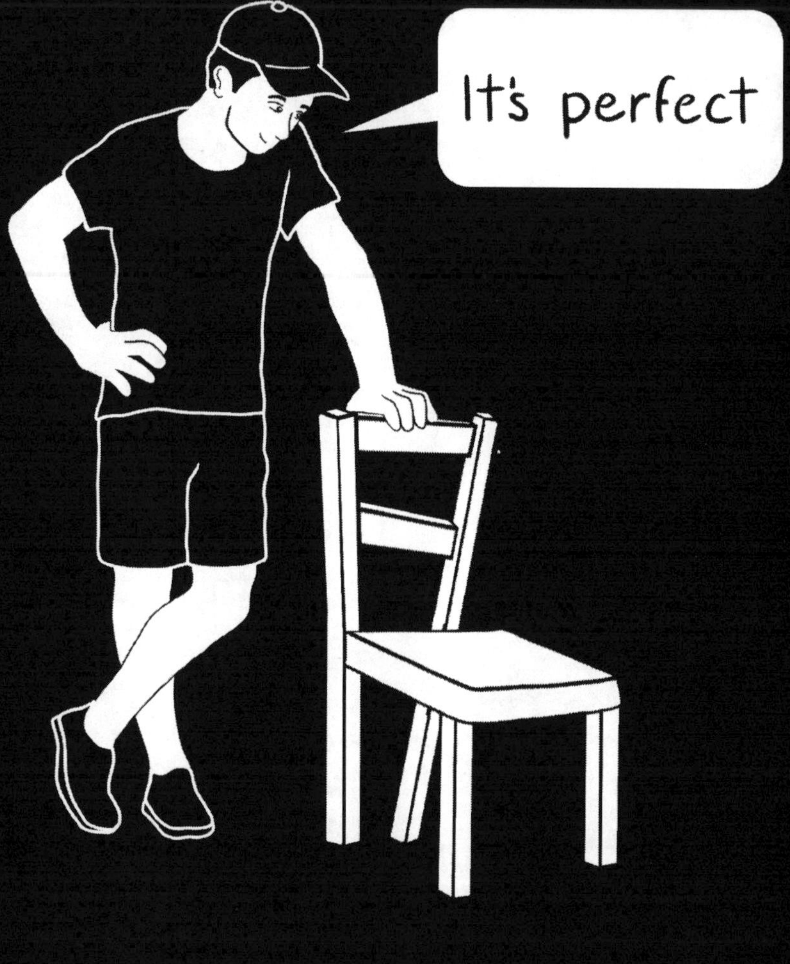
It's perfect

IKEA Effect

People value something more if they've taken part in creating it.

ORIGIN

In 2011, researchers showed that participants were willing to pay more for items they had assembled themselves than for identical pre-assembled products. Their findings showed how personal effort increases perceived value.

EXAMPLES

- **Furniture Assembly:** Consumers often feel a greater attachment to furniture they've built themselves, even if the quality is comparable to professionally assembled pieces.
- **DIY Projects:** Individuals may prefer homemade crafts or meals over store-bought alternatives due to the personal effort invested.

PSA: IKEA, Lego, and Build-a-Bear's business models are all about having us pay for our own labor. lol Imagine if a Lego set came fully assembled.. How pissed would you be?

Pro Tip (Creators): Involving your audience (or patrons) in the creation process can help build a community with a personal investment in your projects.

Halo Effect

When one positive trait influences our entire impression of someone.

ORIGIN

In 1920, psychologist Edward L. Thorndike asked commanding officers to rate subordinates on qualities like intelligence and leadership without meeting them. He found that taller, more attractive servicemen were rated higher overall, leading him to conclude that people tend to let one strong trait shape their entire impression of someone's personality.

EXAMPLE

In a classic 1946 experiment, psychologist Solomon Asch showed participants photos of individuals and asked them to evaluate various personality traits. Participants consistently rated attractive individuals as having more positive traits and unattractive individuals as having the opposite.

The photos were of the **same person.**

Fun Fact: 'The Horn Effect' is the exact opposite of this. Basing your overall impression of someone or something on a single negative characteristic.

He's so Gorgeous!
I'm voting for him!
If I win, I'm making cannibalism legal.
I just feel like I can trust him!

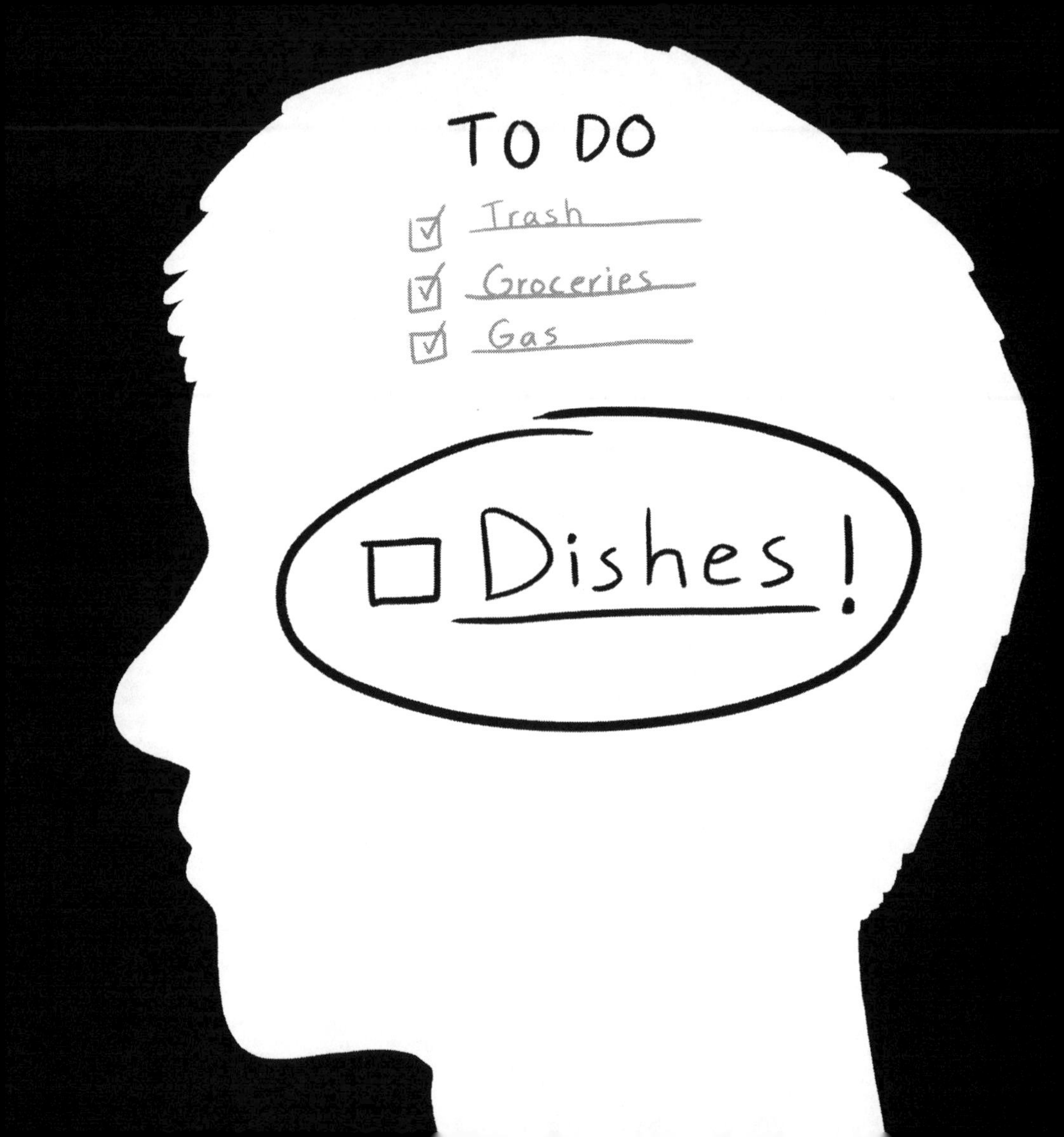
TO DO
Trash
Groceries
Gas
Dishes!

Zeigarnik Effect

People remember unfinished tasks better than completed ones.

ORIGIN

Back in the 1920s, a psychologist named Bluma Zeigarnik noticed that waiters remembered unpaid orders more accurately than those already settled. Naturally, she decided to run some experiments and found that people remember interrupted tasks twice as well as completed ones.

Pro Tip (Content Creators): Want viewers to stick around to the end of a video? Start with a question and don't answer it until the end. What's gonna happen? They gotta watch to find out! You can thank the Zeigarnik Effect for the extra watch time.

This is why cliffhangers at the end of shows work so well. What's gonna happen next? Wait for the next one to find out!

Pro Tip (Morning Strugglers): If you struggle to start your day productively, leave a small task unfinished the night before. The next morning, you'll feel motivated, you'll know exactly where to start, and once you finish it, you'll have momentum to move onto the next thing.

Rashomon Effect

People have different interpretations of the same event, based on their perspectives.

ORIGIN

In 1950, Japanese filmmaker Akira Kurosawa released *Rashomon*, a movie about a crime from multiple conflicting perspectives. The movie showed how personal biases and experiences influence individual accounts of the same incident.

EXAMPLES

1. **Journalism:** Reporters covering the same event may present differing stories based on their viewpoints or the information available to them.
2. **Politics:** Depending on their party affiliation, voters could view a presidential speech as confident, or arrogant.

Nerd Moment: Star Trek TNG - S03 E14 - A Matter of Perspective

In this *Rashomon*-inspired episode, Commander Riker is accused of murder and faces an extradition hearing where everyone's version of what transpired is re-created in the holodeck.

P.S. I added that to the Rashomon Effect Wiki. Picard would be proud.

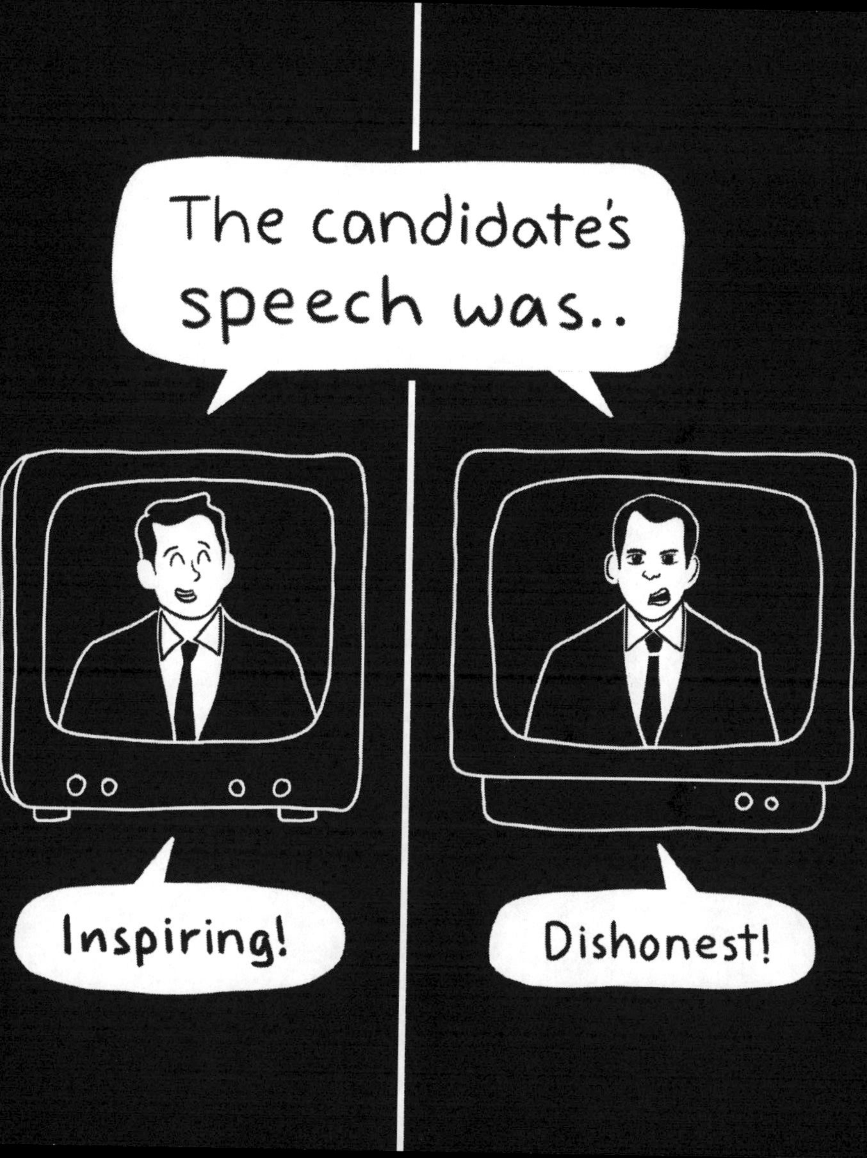
The candidate's speech was..
Inspiring!
Dishonest!

Avg. Annual Salary

Teacher
$40,000

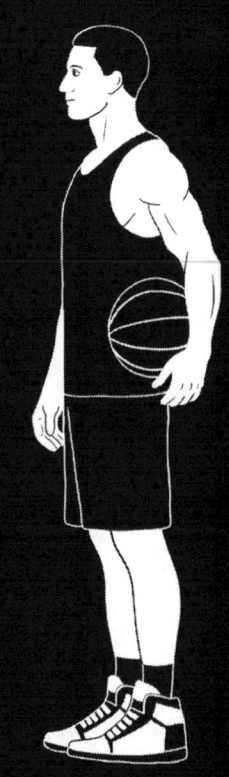

NBA Player
$11,900,000

Paradox of Value

Why some essentials are cheap while luxuries cost a fortune.

ORIGIN

In 1776, economist Adam Smith wrote about how nothing is more useful than water but it lacks value compared to a diamond, which is expensive, but useless. I'd give you the exact quote but honestly.. quotes from the 1700's hurt my brain. It's like everyone just went around talking like Shakespeare. Anyway, the concept goes beyond water and diamonds.

EXAMPLES

- **Gold vs. Iron:** Iron is useful, gold is shiny. While gold has rarity on its side, it doesn't have a lot of practical uses.
- **Entertainment vs. Education:** NBA Players make nearly 300x more money than school teachers annually. Both are important in my opinion but teachers definitely deserve better. Nurses too.
- **Lisinopril vs. Liposuction:** Lifesaving medicines are widely available while cosmetic surgeries are an expensive luxury.

Fact: Modern economists explain this concept with the terms "use value" (how useful it is) and "exchange value" (how much it's worth in the market).

Feynman Learning Technique

Explaining a concept, as if teaching someone else, to deepen your understanding.

ORIGIN

Named after Nobel Prize-winning physicist Richard Feynman, this technique reflects his belief that the best way to grasp a subject is to explain it clearly and simply.

STEPS

1. **Pick a Topic:** Select the topic you want to understand.
2. **Teach it to a Kid:** Explain the concept in super simple language, as if teaching a child.
3. **Identify Gaps:** Figure out where your explanation is unclear.
4. **Simplify and Refine:** Study the material again to fill in the gaps, then adjust your explanation.

EXAMPLE

If you want to understand a bunch of concepts, write a book about them! Write what you think you know (pg. 19), refine your explanation (pg. 102), draw some pictures to help memorize the concepts and then go feed my cats because apparently, you're me making this book.

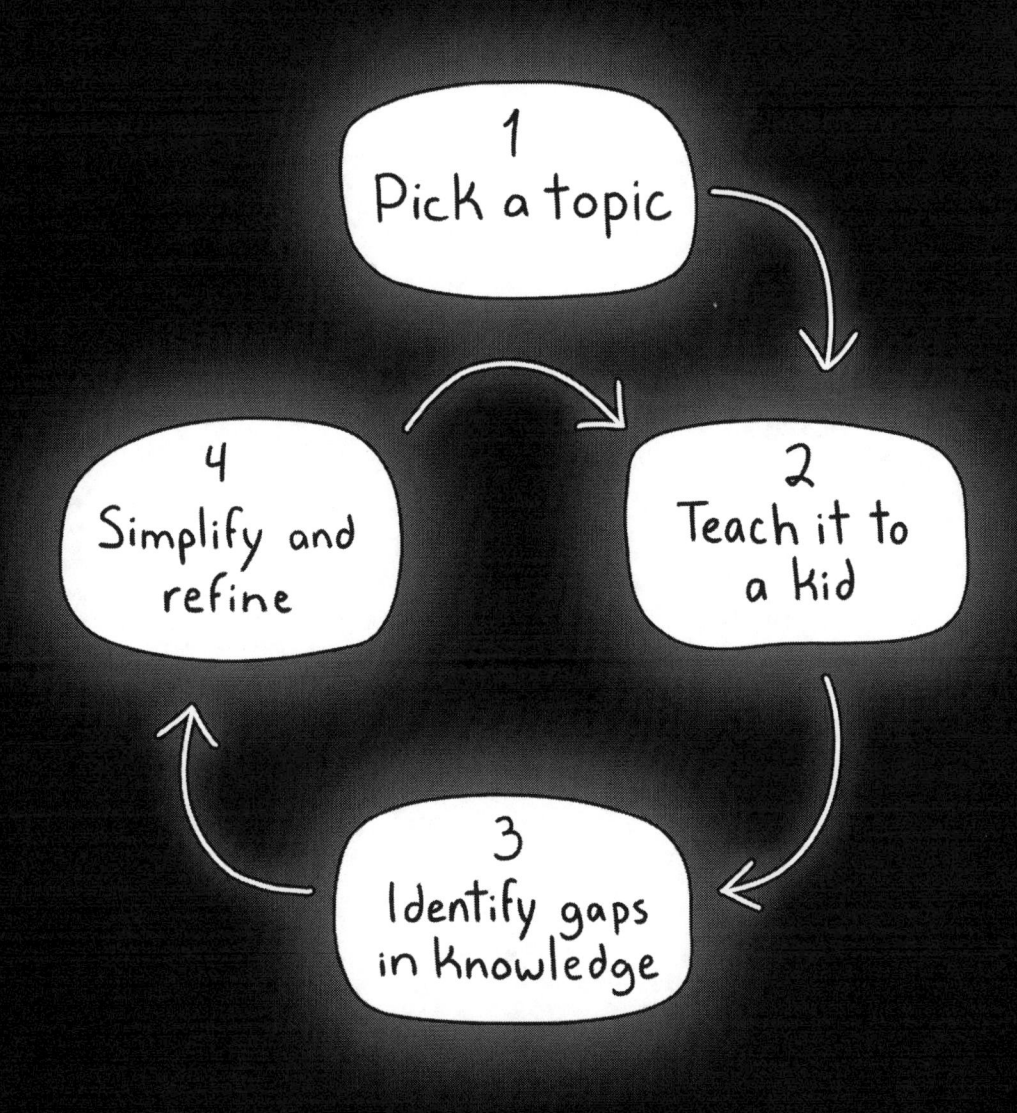

1. Pick a topic
2. Teach it to a kid
3. Identify gaps in knowledge
4. Simplify and refine

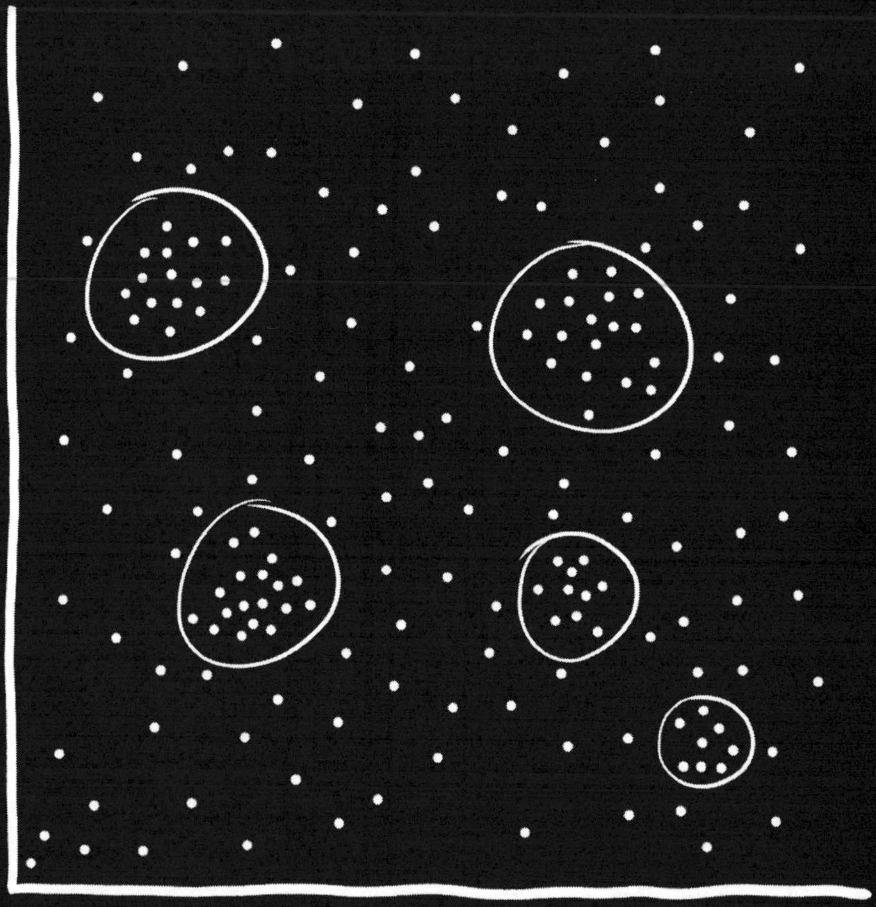

Clustering Illusion

We see patterns in random data, even when there aren't any.

ORIGIN

There are a LOT of sources on this but there isn't really a mind-blowing experiment where the Clustering Illusion originated. Still, psychologists agree that humans tend to see patterns and clusters in random data, like finding shapes in clouds or thinking a coin flip is "due" for heads after a streak of tails. A famous example comes from World War II, when London residents believed V-2 rocket impacts were strategically targeted due to apparent clusters but in 1946, statistician R.D. Clarke revealed the impacts matched a random pattern.

For more in-depth info, look these dudes up.

Thomas Gilovich   *Amos Tversky*   *Robert Vallone*

NOT SO FUN FACT:

In the early 2000s, 12 women working at ABC Studios in Queensland, Australia, had all been diagnosed with breast cancer. 7 of these 12 worked in the same room. After some serious investigation it turned out to just be a coincidence. With enough random data, sometimes patterns emerge by accident.

Google Effect

People are more likely to forget things they can easily look up online.

ORIGIN

In a 2011 study, psychologists Betsy Sparrow, Jenny Liu, and Daniel M. Wegner demonstrated that people tend to forget things that are easily found via search engines. They discovered that when people expect to have future access to information, they're less likely to remember the details themselves. Instead, they remember how to access the information.

EXAMPLES

- **General Knowledge:** The ability to look up things like facts at any moment makes committing them to memory an avoidable task.
- **Phone Numbers:** Let's be honest.. how many do you know? I remember a ton from when I was a kid but today.. maybe like 10? And one of them is 877-CASH-NOW!

DIGITAL AMNESIA

Similar to the Google Effect, *Digital Amnesia* is the tendency to forget things you've stored digitally. For example, I have a swipe-file of YouTube thumbnails for inspiration but I couldn't tell you what any of them look like.

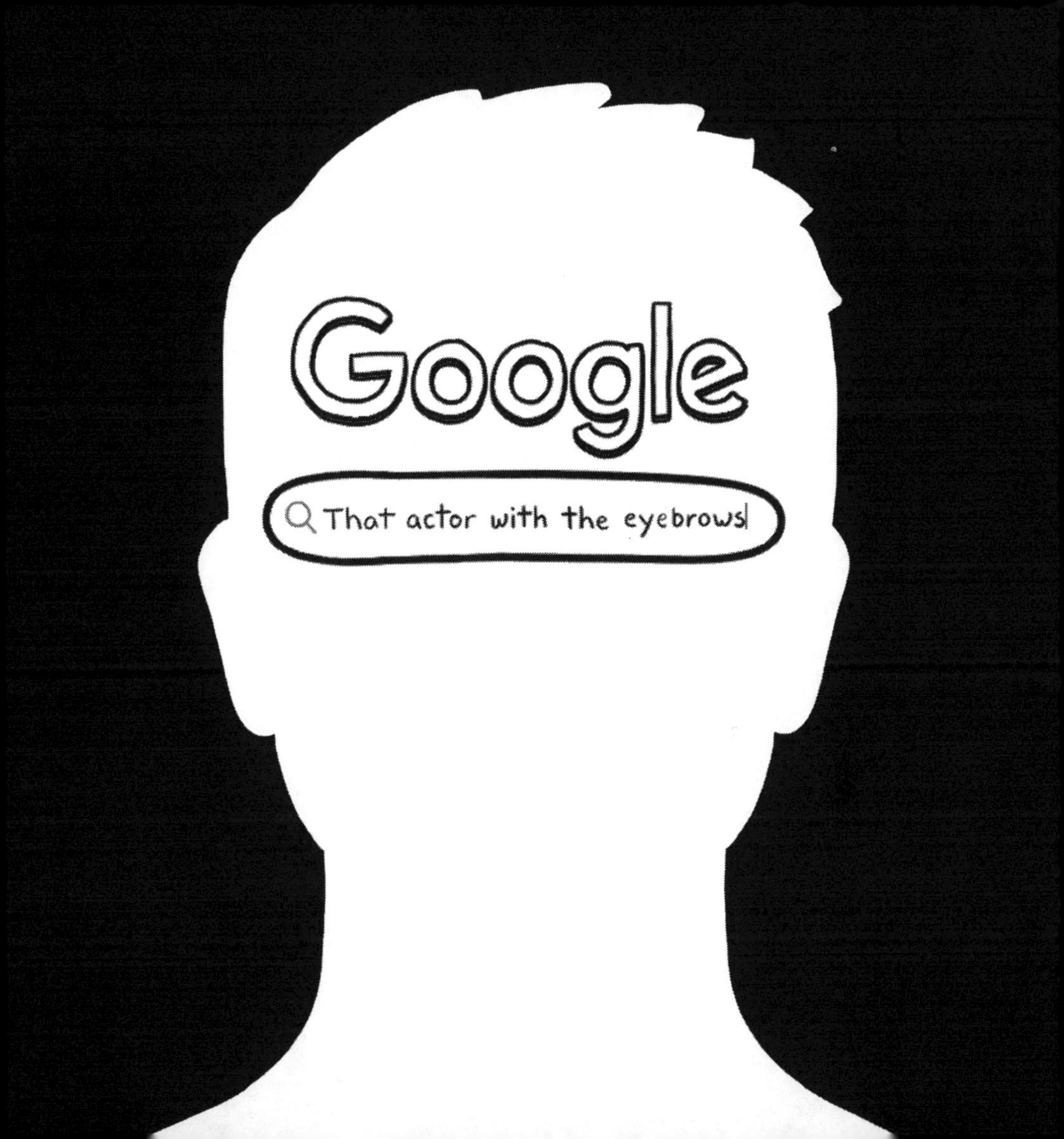
Google
That actor with the eyebrows

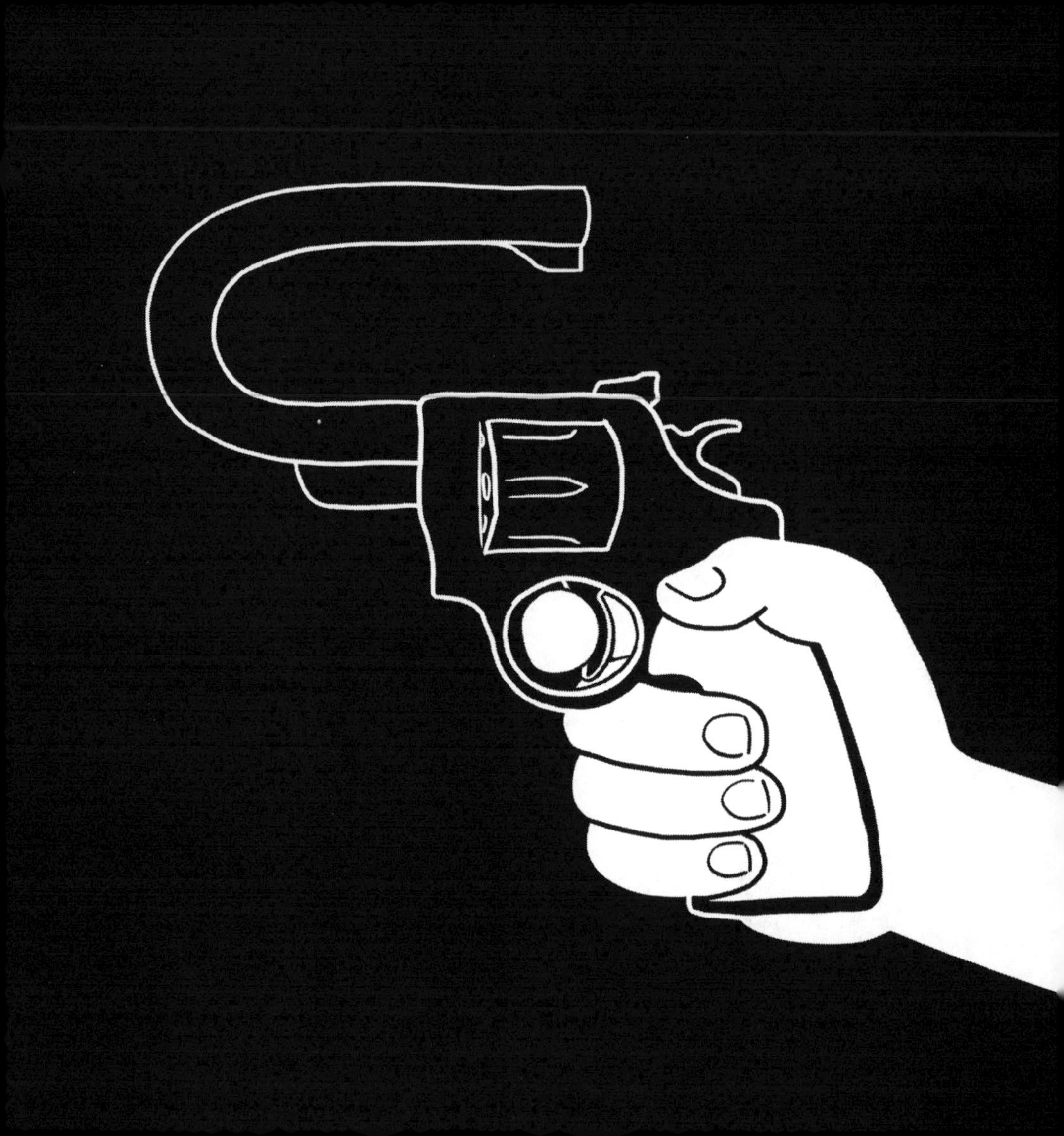

Backfire Effect

When one's beliefs become stronger after they were proven wrong with evidence.

ORIGIN

In 2010, researchers Brendan Nyhan and Jason Reifler conducted experiments on political beliefs to see how people respond to corrections. When participants with strong beliefs were presented with contradictory facts, some **doubled down** on their views instead of changing them.

EXAMPLES

1. Fact-checks from political opponents are more likely to reinforce the misinformation.
2. Correcting myths about the flu vaccine has reinforced them among vaccine skeptics.
3. Attempts to correct conspiracy theories are almost always interpreted as part of the conspiracy.

I'll be honest, when I think of the Backfire Effect, I think.. People believe something - They get proven wrong - Then they act like children.

But in reality, it's mostly observed when the belief is strongly tied to their identity. If change is the goal, picking apart someone's belief system won't get ya there.

Pygmalion Effect

High expectations lead to better performance, while low expectations can lead to worse outcomes.

ORIGIN

The Pygmalion Effect was first identified in the 1960s by psychologists Robert Rosenthal and Lenore Jacobson. In a famous experiment, they told teachers that certain students were expected to show significant intellectual growth based on test results (even though the students were chosen randomly). By the end of the school year, these students had improved more than others, simply because the teachers expected them to.

> **manifestation** *noun*
> 1. the practice of focusing on positive expectations or goals with the belief that this mindset will help bring them into reality.

I personally think the Pygmalion Effect is the key component behind the concept of manifestation. When you believe something strongly, it influences your actions and behavior in ways that help bring it to life, just like high expectations leading to better outcomes.

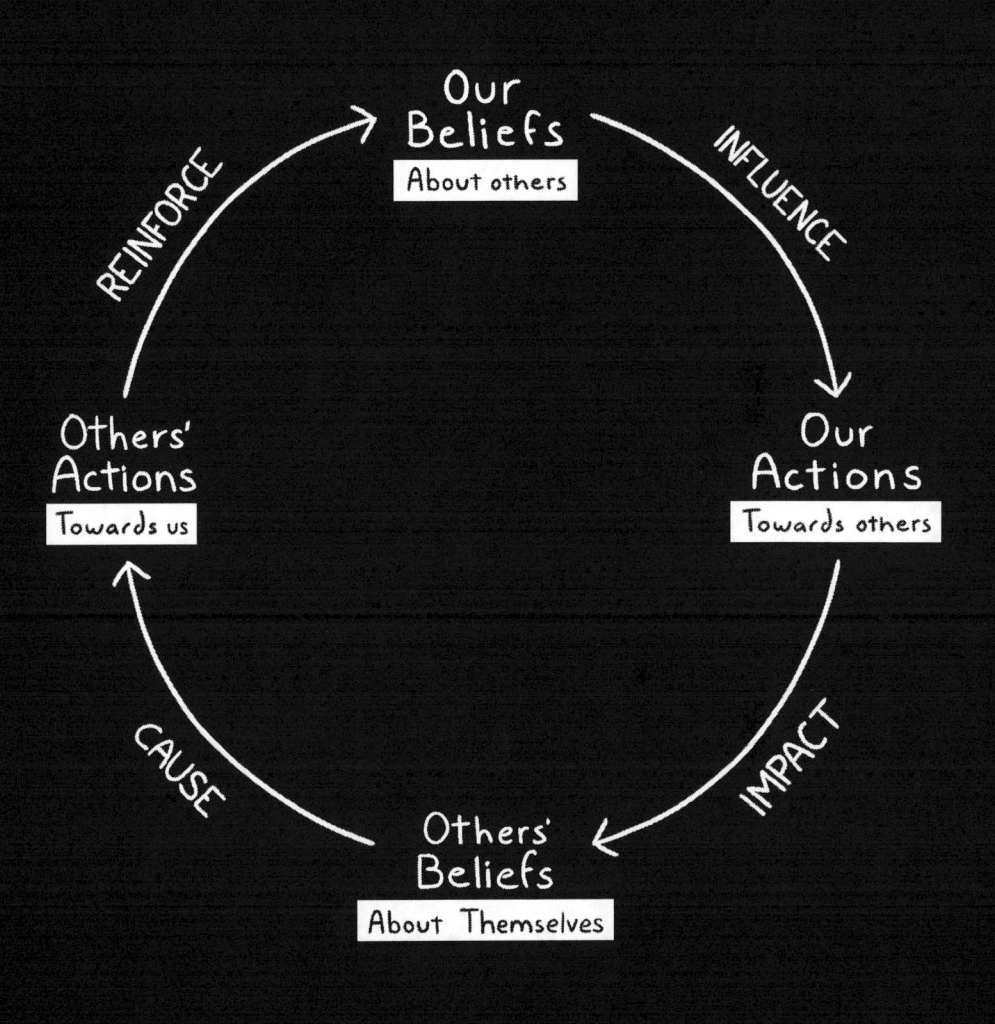

```
            Our
         Beliefs
        About others
  REINFORCE  →  INFLUENCE

  Others'              Our
  Actions            Actions
 Towards us        Towards others

      CAUSE    ←    IMPACT
            Others'
            Beliefs
         About Themselves
```

How much time I said it would take
How much time it ACTUALLY
TOOK
Length of time →

Planning Fallacy

We're way too optimistic about how quickly we can get things done.

ORIGIN

In 1979, psychologists Daniel Kahneman and Amos Tversky noticed that people tend to underestimate the time it takes to complete tasks, even when they have experience with similar projects. This bias happens because we focus on ideal scenarios, ignoring possible setbacks or unexpected delays.

HORMOZI WISDOM

So I was just listening to 100 Million Dollar Leads by Alex Hormozi and he said something that I thought would fit this page perfectly.

*"You can deliver early, but never late. I add 50% to my timeline so I always deliver early, that makes **on time** for me, **early** for them."*

Highly recommend his books by the way, dude knows his stuff.

RELATED ADAGES

Hofstadter's Law: It *always* takes longer than you expect, even when you take into account Hofstadter's Law.

Parkinson's Law: Work expands to fill the time allotted for its completion.

Online Disinhibition Effect

People tend to be more open or aggressive online than they are in person.

ORIGIN

In his 2004 paper *The Psychology of Cyberspace*, psychologist John Suler describes how people behave differently online, becoming either more open (*benign disinhibition*) or more hostile (*toxic disinhibition*), due to several factors.

1. *Anonymity:* The ability to separate online actions from real identity.
2. *Invisibility:* The absence of physical presence and nonverbal cues.
3. *Asynchronicity:* The delay between sending and receiving messages.

COMMON EXAMPLES

1. Twitter Trolls staying anonymous
2. Online gamers screaming racist remarks
3. Redditors safely asking for private advice
4. Introverts in chat talking to a Twitch streamer

The Downfall of Omegle

soundsm.art/omegle

Sad Fact: As of 2023, Approximately 52% of internet users have reported experiencing online harassment.

Confidence Level

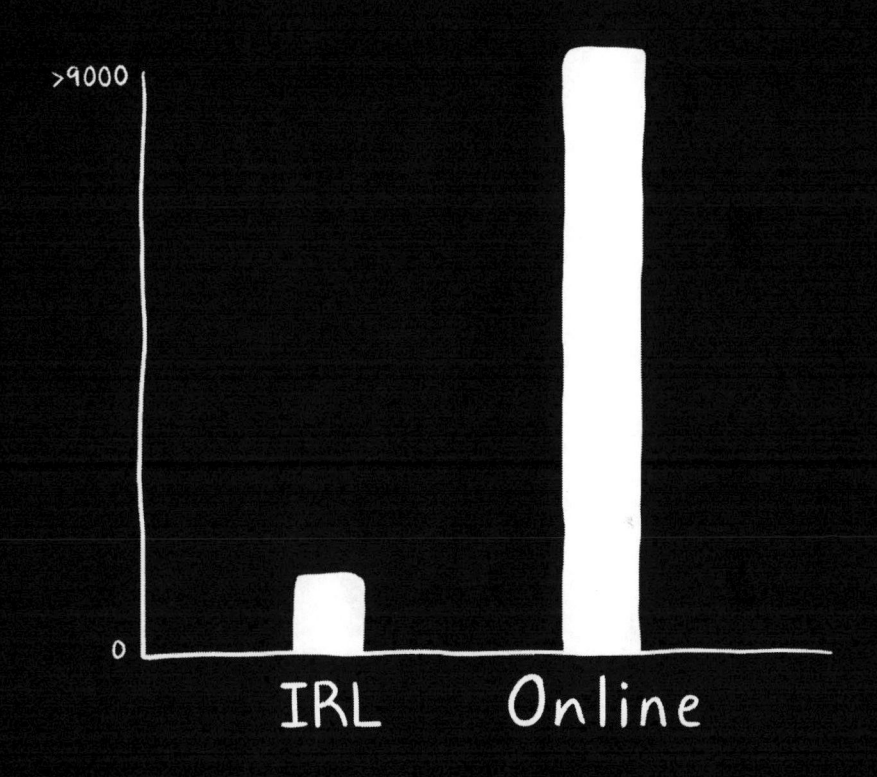

>9000

IRL　　Online

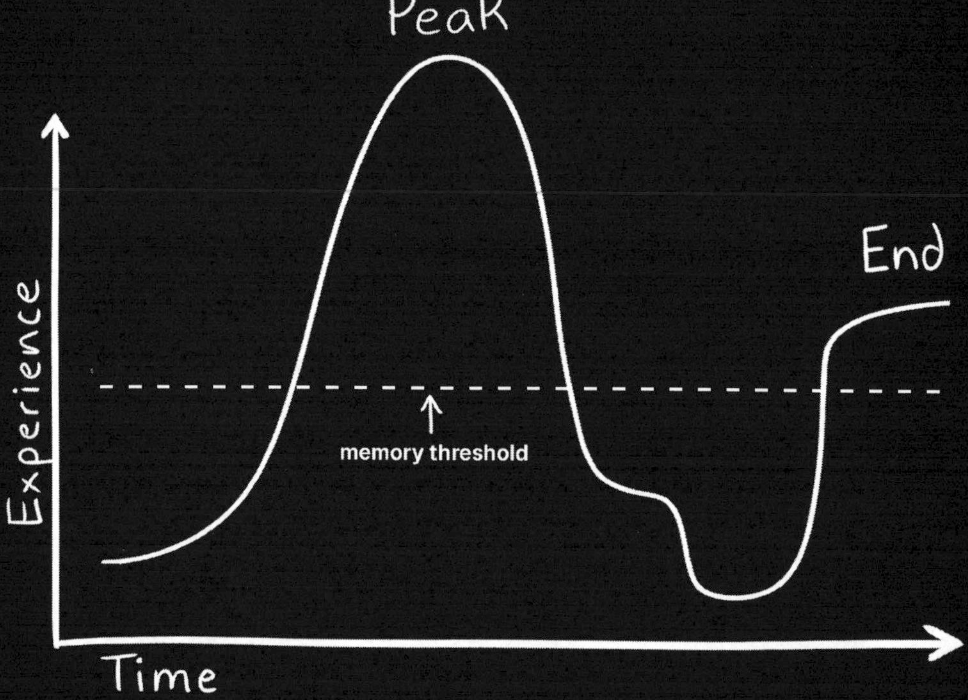

Peak
End
Experience
memory threshold
Time

Peak-End Rule

We remember experiences based on their most intense moment and their end.

ORIGIN

In a 1993 study, Daniel Kahneman and colleagues asked participants to submerge one hand in cold water for 1 min, then the other hand in the same cold water for 1 min plus an additional 30 seconds with slightly warmer water. Participants preferred to repeat the longer trial, because they remembered it not being so bad with the warmer ending.

In a 1996 study, patients rated their pain during colonoscopies. Those with a less painful ending remembered the procedure more positively, even if it took longer overall.

EXAMPLES

Entertainment: Viewers are likely to rate a movie or concert higher if it has a high point (climax) and a satisfying conclusion. (Take note, Creators)

Vacations: People often judge vacations based on standout moments and how they end, rather than the entire experience.

Customer Service: A customer may overlook minor issues during a service interaction if the final moments are handled exceptionally well.

Tsundoku

The act of acquiring books and letting them pile up without reading them.

ORIGIN

The term *tsundoku* originated in 19th century Japan. It combines the words "tsunde-oku" (to pile things up for later) and "dokusho" (reading books), basically capturing the idea of buying books you'll probably never read.

AUTHOR NOTE

Acquiring books can be just as satisfying as reading them, so I appreciate you taking the time to read this one. Here is a list of books that changed who I am as a creator. (not in any particular order)

1. ***Range*** - David Epstein
2. ***Day Trading Attention*** - Gary Vaynerchuk
3. ***Storyworthy*** - Matthew Dicks
4. ***The War of Art*** - Steven Pressfield
5. ***Steal Like an Artist*** - Austin Kleon
6. ***Show Your Work!*** - Austin Kleon
7. ***$100M Offers*** - Alex Hormozi
8. ***$100M Leads*** - Alex Hormozi
9. ***Every Tool's a Hammer*** - Adam Savage

Scan the QR code for quick links to the books.
I will be adding more to the list so ***book***mark it!

Best Books for Creators

soundsm.art/creatorbooks

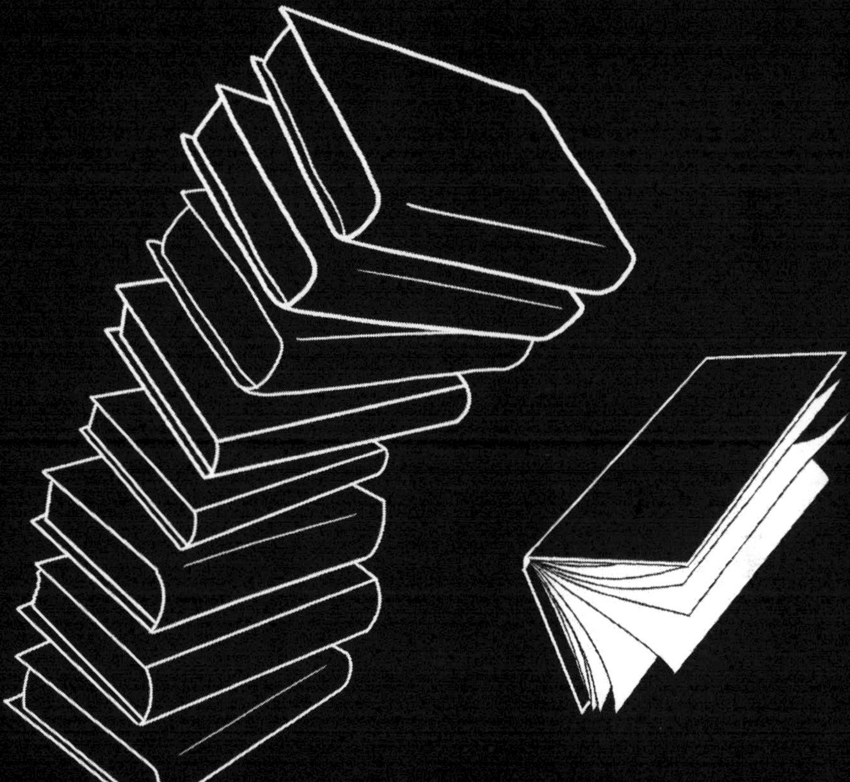

Dimly Lit Bulbs

Concepts that didn't quite make the cut.

Broken Escalator Phenomenon

Even when an escalator isn't moving, people still experience a brief sense of imbalance when stepping onto it.

Maslow's Hierarchy of Needs

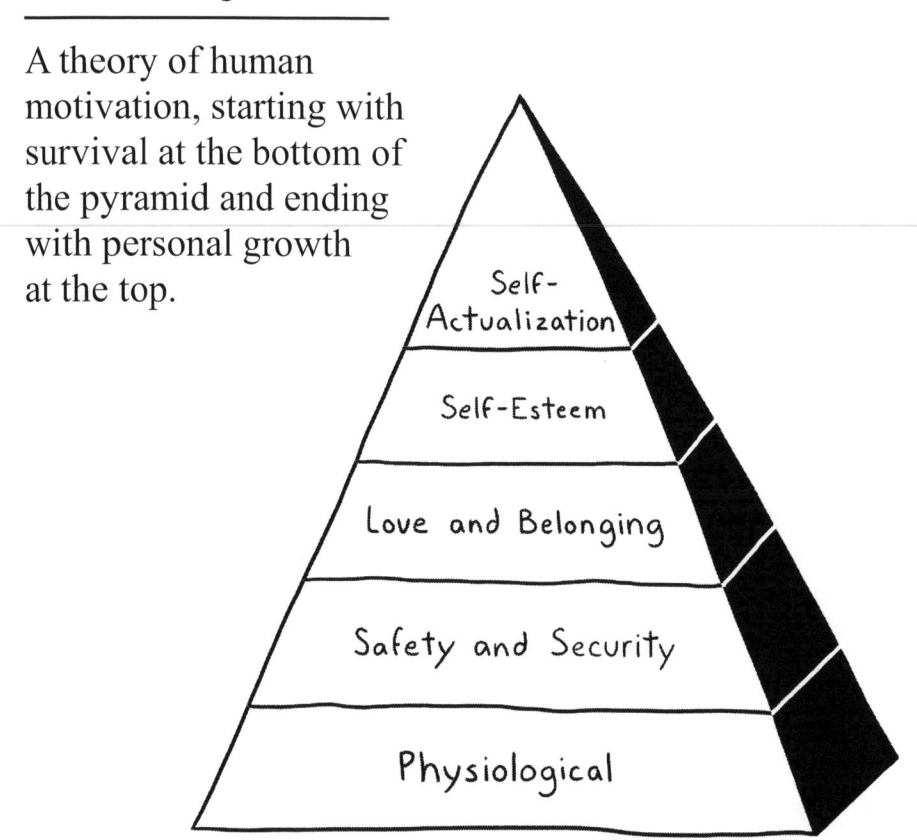

A theory of human motivation, starting with survival at the bottom of the pyramid and ending with personal growth at the top.

- Self-Actualization
- Self-Esteem
- Love and Belonging
- Safety and Security
- Physiological

Proportionality Bias

The tendency to believe that big events must have big causes.

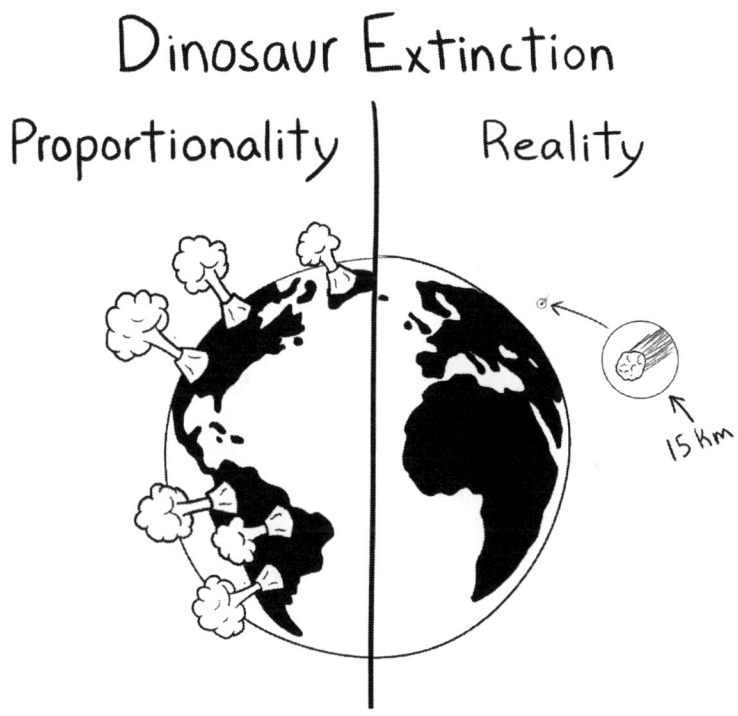

Dinosaur Extinction

Proportionality | Reality

15 km

Prisoner's Dilemma

Two people must decide whether to cooperate or betray each other, with various outcomes depending on their choices.

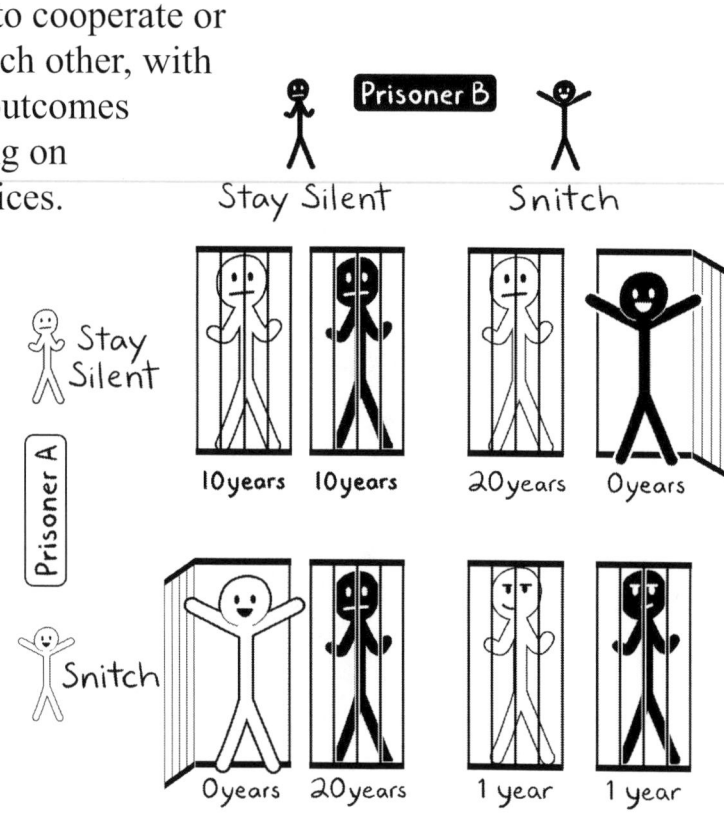

	Prisoner B Stay Silent	Prisoner B Snitch
Prisoner A Stay Silent	10 years / 10 years	20 years / 0 years
Prisoner A Snitch	0 years / 20 years	1 year / 1 year

Present Bias

The tendency to value immediate rewards over future benefits.

SPECIAL THANKS

Nathan Barry

Austin Kleon

Sahil Bloom

Alex Hormozi

Jay Clouse

Gary Vaynerchuk

Mark Manson

David Epstein

Ali Abdaal

THE LIGHTBULB LIST

Through their podcasts, videos, books, blogs, newsletters and threads, the dudes on the left page have all contributed something to this book and my life.

Over the years, I've found myself coming back to specific pieces of content because they offer so much value, so many lightbulb moments, that it can't all be absorbed in one sitting.

Creators who offer that much wisdom in a single piece of content are rare and tough to find, so I've collected the most influential pieces of content in my creator journey, and I'd like to share that with you. I recommend visiting this page once a month to maintain a healthy perspective as a creator and a human being.

soundsm.art/list

REFERENCES

This book shares profound knowledge from *actual* smart people.. I'm just the dude that collected their work, illustrated the concepts, and added a bit of creator perspective. The psychologists, psychiatrists, philosophers, scientists, economists, researchers, and all the other experts mentioned in this book are its true authors and I'm proud to have collaborated with each and every one of them.. even if they don't know about it. (and even if some aren't living)

To explore their original works and the references that inspired this book, scan the QR code or visit the link below.

soundsm.art/references

NOTE FROM THE ~~AUTHOR~~ *Creator*

I can't thank you enough for your support. To be able to create something that someone else actually wants is the best feeling in the world. I loved making this book and hopefully soon, I'll have another for you. (I already have an idea of what I'm doing next.)

Until then, here is a QR code/Link to all the other crap I'm up to.

john.studio

💡 P.S. If you ever watch my videos or livestreams, add a lightbulb emoji to your comment so I know you're family.

Made in the USA
Columbia, SC
31 January 2025